Teaching Preschool Language Arts

Teaching Preschool Language Arts

Lawrence J. Foster   Pauline E. Foster

Brigham Young University Press

Note: Pages in the packet section may be duplicated for nonprofit use.

Library of Congress Cataloging in Publication Data
Foster, Larry, 1901–
　　Teaching preschool language arts.

　　1. Language arts (Preschool) 2. Montessori method of education. I. Foster, Polly, 1919–　　II. Krishnan, Barbara F. III. Title.
LB1140.5.L3F67　　372.6'044　　81-478
ISBN 0-8425-1933-5　　　　　　　AACR2

Library of Congress Catalog Number: 81-478
International Standard Book Number: 0-8425-1933-5
Brigham Young University Press, Provo, Utah 84602
© 1982 Brigham Young University Press. All rights reserved
Printed in the United States of America

10　9　8　7　6　5　4　3　2　1

Preface

Education has made remarkable progress in certain areas of learning. Many young people are receiving excellent training in various fields of science and technology.

However, this positive picture is not consistent throughout all areas of education. Notable is the failure of our elementary, junior, and senior high schools to help young people learn how to read and write, how to spell, and how to understand the language we claim as our national heritage. Year after year some of our high school graduates, even students with college diplomas, enter the commercial world unable to write an acceptable letter of application for a job.

Major industrial and banking personnel directors have complained about this lack of communicative skills. Research on the subject began in 1957 and has continued to the present, and it has not revealed much, if any, noticeable improvement in the problem.

So it was with the desire to find a better way of helping children learn the basic skills of reading, writing, spelling, and understanding language that we began our research in 1959.

Our initial studies led to the discovery of the book *Montessori, Her Life and Work* by E. M. Standing, and our interest was piqued. Continued research led us to England in 1964, where we remained to study this method of education under educators designated by Montessori to train teachers in her method.

In 1973, after several years of experience teaching children and training teachers in the Montessori method, we were invited to join the faculty at the St. Nicholas Training Center in London, where we had received our training.

Returning to the United States in 1977 with the conviction that we had found the program we had been searching for, we began organizing various materials we had obtained from class lectures in London, along with lessons and the reading scheme we had developed there. Many of our classroom observations in British Montessori schools for children are also incorporated into the text. These materials have never before been assembled into a cohesive and usable package for teachers of young children.

Barbara F. Krishnan, artist and Montessori teacher, was invited in 1978 to join us in creating *Teaching Preschool Language Arts*. She is responsible for developing the art concepts.

Contents

Preface v
Introduction: Maria Montessori and Her Influence on Early Childhood Education 1
Implementation of the Montessori Method 7

Section I. The Pink Reading Lab Manual
An Introduction to Parts of Speech: Noun 13
An Introduction to Prewriting and Language 15
    Preparatory Lesson A: Rough and Smooth Boards, One 15
    Preparatory Lesson B: Rough and Smooth Boards, Two 17
    Preparatory Lesson C: Fabric Classification, Rough and Smooth 18
    Preparatory Lesson D: Fabric Matching 20
    Preparatory Lesson E: The Secret Bag 21
    Preparatory Lesson F: Exercises for Pencil Control 23
An Introduction to Writing and Reading 25
    The Three-Period Lesson 27
    Lesson One: Learning the Sounds of the Sandpaper Letters 28
    Lesson Two: Using the Coded Alphabet 31
    Lesson Three: Analysis of Words 33
    Lesson Four: Objects and Word Building 34
    Lesson Five: Noun Game 36
    Lesson Six: Writing 37
    Lesson Seven: Nouns, Box 1 39
    Lesson Eight: Pictured Objects and the Coded Alphabet 41
    Lesson Nine: Objects and Word Cards 43
    Lesson Ten: Large Picture Cards and Word Cards 45
    Lesson Eleven: Loose Picture Cards and Words 47
    Exercise for Pencil Control 48
An Introduction to Grammar 49
    Lesson Twelve: Farm I Nouns 49
    Lesson Thirteen: Verbs, Box 1 51
    Lesson Fourteen: Confusing Words 53
    Lesson Fifteen: Farm I Adjectives 55
    Lesson Sixteen: Pink Word Lists 57
    Lesson Seventeen: Nouns, Singular and Plural 59
    Lesson Eighteen: Farm 1 Verbs 62
    Lesson Nineteen: Definite and Indefinite Articles 64
    Lesson Twenty: Secret Words 66
    Lesson Twenty-One: Verbs, Box 2 68
    Lesson Twenty-Two: Sentences and Pictures 70

Section II. The Blue Reading Lab Manual
Development in Grammar 75
    Lesson One: Longer Nouns 75
    Lesson Two: Exercises for Pencil Control 76
    Lesson Three: Analysis of Words 78
    Lesson Four: Objects for Word Building 80
Progression in Writing and Word Building 81
    Lesson Five: Illustrating and Writing 81
    Lesson Six: Pictured Objects and the Coded Alphabet 82
    Lesson Seven: Objects and Word Cards 84

  Lesson Eight: Large Picture Cards and Word Cards 85
  Lesson Nine: Loose Picture Cards and Word Cards 87
  Lesson Ten: Longer Nouns, Farm One 89
  Lesson Eleven: Verb Commands 90
  Lesson Twelve: Blue Word Lists 92
  Lesson Thirteen: Secret Words 94
 Appendix A: Continued Reading Development 97
 Appendix B: A Compilation of Words Used in This Text 99

Section III. Packet for Colored Materials

Introduction: Maria Montessori and Her Influence on Early Childhood Education

The Beginnings of the Montessori Method

Early in the twentieth century a young psychiatrist, Dr. Maria Montessori, the first woman doctor in Italy, turned from her psychiatric practice to give full attention to the education of the young child.* Her observations of the destructive children in the slums of the San Lorenzo district in Rome led her to believe that something other than her services as a doctor was needed.

As a result of her observations, Dr. Montessori began preparing materials that eventually became known as the didactic objects in the "prepared environment." The living environment was her laboratory. By the simple process of observation she was able to ascertain which pieces of material continued to hold a child's attention. Those that failed were modified successfully or discarded. In this manner, she completed a curriculum of didactic materials that began to be used for children from three to six years of age.

The first Montessori school, the *Casa de Bambini,* was opened in one of the very tenements where destruction had been taking place. Dr. Montessori's fame grew quickly. The *Casa de Bambini* soon became known to educators in many countries. They came to see her children and went away amazed at the abilities they displayed.

One day Dr. Montessori was ill and didn't appear to open the school. Visitors came and found the little ones at work. A child had climbed through the open transom and had opened the door for the other children. They went to work. The visitors were amazed to see the busy, active children functioning without anyone telling them what to do. These were the same children who, a few months earlier, had been destructive.

Dr. Montessori was invited to lecture in many countries of the world. Her lectures in the United States were attended by enthusiastic crowds that filled auditoriums from coast to coast. No one knows why she refused an offer by William McClurg, the publisher, to set up her own training center in the United States.

Montessori education flourished in the United States in the areas where she had lectured. However, Dr. Montessori had left no one in the United States to continue the training, and after a number of years, Montessori schools were hard to find.

With the advent of faster and less expensive ocean travel, followed soon by not too expensive and even faster air travel, Montessori-trained teachers began to revive the Montessori method in the United States. Beginning in the late 1950s and early 1960s, interest in Montessori education renewed and has steadily grown. Today Montessori schools are to be found from coast to coast. Training courses for teachers are offered by established Montessori organizations, universities, and colleges.

Dr. Montessori wrote many books on observations of children and the method she had designed. She left the world a legacy of innovative ideas on how children developed, how they should be freed to learn, and when the learning should begin. Other well-known educational thinkers have set forth their philosophies on education. However, Dr. Montessori not only set forth her theory and philosophy in a clear and concise manner but also designed a complete method of education, including the materials that accompanied that method.

Maria Montessori attributed much of her early philosophy and theory to the teachings of Edouard Seguin, a noted French scientist who had worked successfully with deaf mutes. She was so influenced by Seguin that she devoted

---

*Information for this introduction is taken largely from Maria Montessori's *The Absorbent Mind,* published in London at the Theosophical Publishing House in 1969 (pp. 125–166).

two years, 1898 to 1900, to the education of handicapped children. This influence is further seen in Montessori's use of the Seguin boards, fully accredited to him. She also gave Seguin full credit for the development of the "three-period lesson" plan, used throughout her curriculum.

Dr. Maria Montessori's Theory and Philosophy Concerning Language Arts

Maria Montessori did not believe that reading, writing, spelling, and language should be taught as separate entities. Her contention was that these subjects should be presented as a whole idea at the time a child indicated readiness. The Montessori teacher, often referred to as "the servant of the child," is the main aid in effecting learning when the child has reached the stage known in Montessori philosophy as the "golden moment." The ability to observe the child and to know when to present information for each step in his learning is considered to be just as important as, if not more than, knowing how to present each Montessori lesson. Developing the power of observation, the Montessori teacher not only learns what the precise *moment* is for presenting each step of learning but also comes to understand the value of presenting it *in its proper sequence.* The child, as a result, is the victor instead of the victim in his attempt to become master of his environment.

It was Montessori's thesis that not only were most children ready to learn at a much earlier age than had been previously thought, but that learning was also a child's right and something he really wanted to do. Furthermore, the environment she designed was to be a place where the child could enjoy working as he pursued goals that stemmed from an innate desire to be industrious.

Montessori made it clear to all who came to see her young ones, aged three to five, that these children not only were ready to learn but that no other period in their lives offered them the opportunity to learn so effectively. Maria Montessori called this period the *sensorial* period and taught that sensorial development began at the moment of birth. It was Montessori's contention that certain of these sensorial developments had their beginnings during the prenatal stage. Modern psychologists have since confirmed her findings.

This sensorial period, which Montessori referred to as the optimum time for a child's learning through the use of his senses, is not to be considered the same for each child. Each step of readiness will vary with the individual child.

Montessori discovered that most children are ready to begin entry into the prepared environment at around age three. She also discovered that this optimum developmental period continues for about four years. As these sensorial abilities begin to diminish, they are replaced by another type of learning, when children are around age seven. At this stage, the intellect takes over. As a result of a child's successful learning experience in the prepared environment, all learning becomes much easier. The child begins to realize, probably for the first time, that he is the learner. Montessori found, furthermore, that the child who has been able to develop his sensorial abilities properly faces the problem of ambiguity—long the despair of both teachers and students—with complete confidence in his ability to solve the problems of the classroom and eventually of life itself.

The readiness of a three-year-old to learn how to read, write, spell, and understand the complexities of the English language has its beginnings shortly after birth. No one knows when all the sensorial abilities begin to manifest themselves. At age two months, when the infant begins to turn his head at the sound of a voice, he begins to go through well-established periods of development until at age two he is able to express himself, using almost all parts of speech in a verbal explosion.

It was Montessori's theory that between age one and two the child needs people who will talk to him intelligently without baby talk. Watching the lips of those who talk to him as well as listening to the sound of their voices, the child learns to construct his sentences and acquires vocabulary. "We must come to understand," Montessori said, "that the child reaches his knowledge by himself;

but that is no reason for our not speaking to him grammatically or for not helping him to construct his sentences."

At about a year and a half the child discovers another fact: that each thing has its own name. "This shows," Montessori said, "that from all the words he has heard, he has been able to single out the nouns, and especially the concrete nouns." At this stage the child enters a period in which he uses single words to take the place of sentences. These are called *fusive words* or sometimes *portmanteau words.* For example, upon seeing his supper being prepared, the little child says, "Mupper," meaning, "Mummie, I want some supper."

This short period is quickly followed by the use of two-word phrases, each word standing for many. Soon after this, at around age two, an immense verbal explosion occurs in which a multitude of new words comes into use—hundreds of nouns, prepositions, verbs, and adjectives. As we stated earlier, and it cannot be stressed too emphatically, the child's ability at this stage to use his command of verbal expression will be directly related to the vocabulary he has been listening to up to this period.

Two other important factors are necessary to an understanding of the child's readiness to enter into the next phase of learning. These very important factors, known in Montessori education as *movement* and the *use of the hand,* had their beginnings much earlier in the child's life. Considering each of these separately will aid in understanding their value to the child's development.

Traditionally the role of movement in school life, especially during the developmental period, has been assigned to physical education, exercise, or games—with little or no thought given to its close connection with the developing mind.

Among the many new educational ideas Montessori developed was the theory that brain, sense, and muscle (the "system of relationship") should be used as an integral whole to put man in touch with his world. "One of the greatest mistakes of our day," said Montessori, "is to think of movement by itself as something apart from the higher functions. To give them their right place, man's movements must be coordinated with the center—the brain."

It was Montessori's contention that all educators up to her time had thought of movement and the muscular system as aids to respiration, or circulation, or as means for building up physical strength. "But in our new conception," she said, "the view is taken that movement has great importance in mental development itself, provided that the action which occurs is connected with the mental activity going on."

Montessori believed that movement helps the development of the mind, and this development finds renewed expression in further movement and activity. "It follows," she related, "that we are dealing with a cycle, because mind and movement are parts of the same entity." She believed that the senses also take part, and that the child who has less opportunity for sensorial activity remains at a lower level.

This book amply demonstrates these two characteristics of early childhood development: purposeful movement and sensorial input. In line with Montessori's ideas on movement, she considered the two-year-old well able to walk distances of one or two miles, but, she said, "It is we who must go at his pace." This participation in movement and the educational benefits to be derived from it are enhanced by patient explanation of everything the child sees as he walks.

A thorough consideration of Dr. Montessori's theory and philosophy on the development of the hand and the influence of movement on the intellect would require many more pages than is possible here. We will therefore condense the information to the extent possible.

Starting (a) at about age four months when the infant studies his own hands and begins the development of grasping, he passes through successive stages of hand development, as follows: (b) nine months: selected grasping; (c) one year: work repetition, practice, and discrimination between desires; (d) fifteen months: first activities of the hand directed toward work, lifting heavy objects, climbing; (e) twenty months to two years: working with hands, cleaning, dusting, moving things with a purpose, and setting the table.

Although formal learning in a Montessori school generally begins at age three, today many young ones come to Montessori schools at age 2½. The prepared environment affords these children the opportunity not only of solidifying gains already made but also of working with some of the practical life materials in preparation for the start of formal learning at age three.

At this point a brief discussion of Dr. Montessori's theory and philosophy as applied to the "prepared environment" is necessary to enable the reader to understand better Montessori's format for the best possible conditions for learning. Foremost is her theory that the lessons be given on an individual basis. This format is carried on throughout the Montessori curriculum with very few exceptions. These exceptions occur when the lesson lends itself to an activity that necessarily involves several children. The Montessori format for the individual lesson is based on the three-period lesson plan originated by Edouard Seguin. The material is presented to a child at the indicated step of readiness.

The care and use of the prepared environment is itself an effective teacher in helping the child learn to respect the rights of others and in helping her to develop order in her world. Following is the Montessori format for use of the materials:

- The child may work with any material that has been shown her.
- The child may work with the material as long as she uses the material in the manner demonstrated.
- No other child may interfere or invade her working area unless invited to do so.
- All material must be placed back on the shelf by the user exactly as she found it.
- No material may be passed on to another child.

Self-discipline is another important part of Dr. Montessori's philosophy. It was her belief that the only true discipline is self-discipline. She also believed that this kind of discipline results when the child is given—within certain limits—the freedom to effectively advance her own development. Permissiveness, according to Dr. Montessori, is destructive to a child's development and should never be used. In the Montessori philosophy, an important and difficult aspect of the teacher's role in the classroom is suppressing such behavior and replacing it with constructive attitudes of what is right.

These rules in the prepared environment are few, but they are effectively and strictly enforced. They do provide limits and guidelines for the child attempting to adjust to new social and intellectual experiences. Montessori saw the period of birth to age three as one of unconscious learning. At age three the period of conscious learning takes over in the form of two developmental operations. First, the child now begins to use all those powers which, up to now, he has been developing. As Dr. Montessori so aptly put it, "Being able now to tackle his environment deliberately and consciously, he begins a period of real constructiveness." The other kind of development consists in perfecting the acquisitions already made. Language is a very clear example because it continues until around age six.

This age of perfecting and enriching those powers already formed are now assisted by the hand, which becomes a prehensile organ of the mind. It was Dr. Montessori's thesis alone that the hand was the instrument of the mind. In the new kind of environment she developed, children were encouraged to use their freedom within limits and to use their hands in that environment.

The preparation for writing takes place through the use of specially designed apparatus for helping the child learn to control his movements in the environment and for practicing his powers of sensorial discrimination. Dr. Montessori called this the principle of *indirect preparation*.

Based on Montessori's theory and philosophy of learning, we have constructed *Teaching Preschool Language Arts* in such a manner that it is now possible to assist children in the total language-arts field according to her beliefs.

Implementation of the Montessori Method

We present this code-cracking, linguistic approach to the difficult problems of teaching all the components of language arts in a manner allowing reading, writing, spelling, grammar, and composition to become parts of a unified discipline. We recognize the need for an integrated linguistic approach to the many problems facing educators today also the need for curriculum materials that will enable this kind of a program to be easily implemented with built-in, positive feedback for both the teacher and the learning child. This program, as presented, is appropriate for Headstart, preschools, kindergarten, first grade, and second grade. It is basically a two-year program for the preschool child, but if it is begun at age six, it will normally be completed within a year.

Because of its integrated approach, this text can also be used for remedial work as well as for teaching English as a second language. While its main focus is on school use, its lessons and materials have been so constructed that they can be used at home by parents concerned with a child's progress in the aforementioned areas.

This book is presented in two sequential sections, the Pink Lab Manual and the Blue Lab Manual, each with its accompanying materials. The lesson plans, the instructions for preparation, and the accompanying materials have been precisely coded for proper identification and use.

The formats for the Pink and Blue Lab Manuals provide the teacher with explicit instructions for giving each lesson, all the pertinent materials for the system, and instructions for assembling that material. The material is sequentially organized according to the level of difficulty; the lesson plans are carefully constructed for each specific lesson, and the philosophy related to the pacing of the lesson is presented clearly and concisely. **Format**

The lessons in the lab manual are presented in the following order: **Order**

- The lesson plan for using the material
- Instructions for preparing the material for the lesson
- Material to be prepared for the lesson

It is imperative that the teacher be able to evaluate the readiness in each phase of the material before going on to the next step. Under no circumstance is the material to be presented out of sequence. Failure to observe this basic principle will result not only in confusing the child but also in a loss of basic skills that become critical—a loss that will hamper the child's later learning development and confidence in himself. This kind of interruption of sequential learning, more than any one factor, is responsible for the many failures of general reading programs. **Note**

The Pink Lab Manual

The first lab section, the Pink Manual, is strictly structured as to the level of difficulty and introduces the child to the following elements:

- Indirect preparation materials for later intellectualized development, including practical life and sensorial development
- The early use of grammar

Grammar is introduced very early in the child's school life. All elements of grammar receive a color-coding at the beginning of the system, and these colors remain static throughout the entire language-arts program. Nouns, on black cards, are introduced first, the child receiving his own name card on his first day of school. Using the system, he is progressively exposed to further elements of grammar. During his phonetic reading development, he learns the functions of the following:

    nouns: black
    verbs: red
    adjectives: dark blue
    articles: light blue

- The beginning lessons in the techniques that help the child learn to read

In these lessons the child uses and develops the kinesthetic sense that is such a definite aid in a young child's learning. This sense development has long been neglected and little understood in the teaching of normal children. It has been used only to teach children with learning difficulties and even then very seldom.

- The introduction of materials for learning the initial code-cracking techniques

These are the phonetic sounds of the letters of the alphabet. The term *phonetic* means that only one sound is assigned to one letter, no matter what position that letter may have in a word. These are the unchanging sounds.

Rationalization for the Method

1. Teaching the individual versus the group is a superior teaching method. The human organism is so constructed that no one human being can ever think or reason exactly as does another. Historically, U.S. mass educational systems have accepted the thesis that large numbers of children can be taught only in homogeneous groups that have come to mean grouping according to age. There is no longer much attempt to group according to ability. Laws have been enacted recently in an attempt to reverse this trend, to protect the right of the individual to freedom to learn as fast as he will. Unfortunately, school systems at the present time have few materials and little or no knowledge of how to implement the individualized approach demanded by such laws.

2. *Teaching Preschool Language Arts* is based on the philosophy that the individual's needs can be met whether on an individualized basis or as an individual within a group.

3. Rules of grammar can be fun and can become an exploratory experience if taught early and in a concrete manner. Through repeated activity in the environment with the grammar materials provided in these lab manuals, the child integrates his knowledge of the function of grammar.

4. The exercises allow the child to develop the large and small muscle skills necessary for excellent handwriting while allowing freedom for the child to

develop his own style. At the same time, development of hand-eye coordination and the left-to-right eye movement necessary for reading and writing skills grow with amazing speed. These writing skills are developed in a manner that allows letter formation in the early years to lead to a natural cursive writing, not requiring the child to learn first to print and then to unlearn those techniques in order to perfect cursive skill.

5. The phonetic approach to reading is consistent. The child learns easily that which he can count upon to remain consistent. A three-letter phonetic approach to reading—in which each letter in the word stands for only one unvarying sound regardless of its position—answers this need of the young, untaught child. Consistency in the way to crack the code that allows him to learn English in a logical, nonthreatening manner acts as a spur to his desire for learning to read. All children have this desire, regardless of race or intellectual ability. It is only when faced with undecipherable obstacles that they become convinced they are unable to cope and retire into nonlearning. In this system, three-letter phonetic words are presented more than once in a variety of interesting ways. Presentation is first, with the concrete materials the child may handle and observe, followed by increasingly abstract techniques. The child comes to realize the theoretical representation of the sound that composes words, then the function of the word that represents the concrete concept.

6. Spelling becomes a natural development. As the child begins to gain knowledge and to internalize the abstraction of the symbol representing the sound, spelling follows naturally. He uses his sensory development to reproduce the symbol that represents the sound. He often learns to write these symbols before he learns to read.

7. Composition also follows naturally. Within this program a child is given many opportunities to express himself. His first expression probably will come through his art experiences. Soon, he is able to dictate to a supporting teacher the action his pictured art represents. The teacher records his words on the drawing, written in the manner the child is learning. He will later imitate these letters. The teacher encourages the child to identify the objects in his picture he wishes to write about, aiding him when he cannot reproduce the sounds he needs, spelling and writing for him words that are not phonetic. She encourages him to reproduce all the sounds he is able to, allows him to write them in an unstructured, nonthreatening environment. These parts of grammar are reintroduced several times during this early reading stage. All the words are three-letter phonetic words, and all are color-coded.

8. Farm one reintroduces elements of grammar. Through the use of small farm animals the child more firmly establishes elements of grammar. First he is given the noun cards to place beside each animal with a phonetic name. The other parts of speech suitable to his level are introduced at proper intervals. The child manipulates the cards to form descriptive sentences or phrases about the objects in the farm. At the same time he is internalizing the structure of syntax. At this time he is free to write or not to write the sentences he has composed.

The Blue
Lab Manual

The second lab section is the Blue Lab Manual, with the materials coded blue and pegged to a level of expanding reading difficulty. The Blue Lab Manual continues with the same format as the Pink Lab Manual. This format consists of the five areas: reading, writing, spelling, grammar, and composition.

1. *Reading*

The techniques the child has learned in using the sequential materials in the Pink Reading Lab are enhanced and developed in this set of materials. She is led to the knowledge that she now has the skill to tackle much longer words. Again, she is guided gently from the concrete use of material into abstraction. All materials on this level remain completely phonetic but are now much expanded from the three-letter limit of her beginning experience.

2. *Handwriting*

The child is introduced to slightly more complicated design work involving the development of muscular skills necessary for pencil control. She is also introduced to writing paper constructed with a two-color writing guide. This is the beginning of gentle encouragement to refine her letters in order to fit them to the modules indicated by the paper. She is encouraged also to record the word, phrase, or sentence she has composed with the movable alphabet or the grammar cards she uses each day.

3. *Spelling*

The child now uses concrete objects and pictures to spell longer words. She uses word cards to check her efforts to spell these names of objects. The child's work is the result of her choice. This freedom to choose results in sustained interest. She works longer at a task, with infinitely better results because the task is self-chosen rather than imposed. At this time the teacher begins to dictate and the child to write longer phonetic words. The teacher will point out the letters the child forms very well for his level of competency at pencil control. This gives him a model to work toward. She at no time criticizes the child's work, although he may.

4. *Grammar*

Longer phonetic words are added to the four parts of grammar the child is already using with the farm. Phonetic verb command cards, demanding more than one action, are added to the room environment.

5. *Composition*

The child begins to write his own stories instead of telling them verbally to the teacher. He is now introduced to the use of his first picture dictionary. If the child is unable to find a word he needs, the teacher will write it out on a paper for him. All unphonetic words are supplied in this manner as the child seeks to improve his dictionary skills. The teacher will note that the blue material is developed exactly as was the pink material, the only difference being the length of the phonetic words the child uses, with additional emphasis upon letter size and position on the two-color coded handwriting paper. In the pink materials the child is required to read half-inch modules. His handwriting is completely unstructured. In the blue materials the reading modules decrease to three-eighths of an inch, and the child must begin attempting to bring his handwriting forms down to the half-inch modules of his first writing paper. He now learns to space his words on the paper.

Section I.

The Pink Reading Lab Manual

An Introduction to Parts of Speech: Noun

Materials

One set of black name cards containing the names of all the children in the room.

- Print the names in white ink on black strips, 5½ inches by 2 inches.
- Write the letters in cursive script.
- Write the letters large, on half-inch modules.
- Contact the cards front and back with clear plastic.
- Draw guidelines to keep the letters consistently the same size.

Philosophy

Young children are very interested in the nature of words. They love to know that certain words embody the idea of person, place, thing, and feeling and that other words tell how these nouns act.

This text uses children's natural fascination with words to teach the functions of the parts of speech. Children need never relearn these functions at a later time when their early interests have been replaced by others.

Procedure

From the first day a child is in the room, give him (or her) his own name card. He may use this card for any number of activities, such as

- putting the card on the table at which he wishes to sit.
- laying the card on the mat where he is working.
- putting the card at his chosen place to sit on the conference ellipse (part of the teacher-prepared environment).

As teacher, also use the card in many ways from the first day:

- Hold up the card to call a child to your side.
- Hold up the card to dismiss a child.
- Display the card to indicate a child's turn in a group game.
- Place the card to indicate a child's assigned place.
- Display the card to indicate that a child may do a necessary task.
- Use the card in other ways convenient for the children.

As a result of this activity, the children will soon be reading each others' names, particularly if you begin the practice when they are about three. Younger children show a surprising facility when they are exposed to this technique.

Do not introduce the idea of *noun* in the beginning work with names in the room.

An Introduction to Prewriting and Language

Preparatory Lesson A:
Rough and Smooth Boards, One

Materials
- the prepared pink board (see instructions following Preparatory Lesson B)
- the child's table

Philosophy

The first steps of the readiness method concern the sensitivity of a child's fingertips and the proper cultivation of this sensitivity toward aiding her development and learning.

The sense of touch can be the basis for the proper development of all the other senses. It is certainly one young children strive to develop. Anyone who observes a young child for a time will recognize the need of that child to touch, to hold, to stroke, to squeeze, to experience every object she sees.

This striving to know through touching begins to dull if she does not receive careful training before she becomes too old. It is still present and may be cultivated early in a child's school life. At three, she has full potential for continuing development. At six, however, she has begun to lose the ability to learn through touch and soon thereafter must depend upon her intellect for learning. She never learns as easily as she would have if the sense of touch been developed early.

Procedure

Taking the pink board to the child's table, explain that you wish to show her some work. Place the board on her table; then take her to the area where she washes her hands. This can be the normal area, such as the washbasin in the restroom, or an area prepared in the classroom with washbasin, soap, water, and towels.

Show her how to wash her hands. Do this in a gentle manner, using a lot of suds, plunging her soaped hands into a basin of warm water to rinse, and drying the hands and the fingertips very gently.

Returning to the table, sit with the child and gently pick up her hand. (Your responsibility is to learn whether she is right- or left-handed.) Have her extend her first and second fingers; then place her two fingers upon the smooth card of the pink board. Gently move her fingers from left to right across the surface of the card. Repeat this movement until the child gets the idea and continues by herself.

Say, "Smooth," repeating the word as her fingers move across the surface. Give the child time to repeat the word after you. When she does, take her hand again and move it gently across the smooth side of the board, always from left to right.

Repeat the above procedure with the rough card of the pink board. Repeat the word "rough" until the child says it after you. Remove the child's hand from the board and say: "Show me rough." If she does, follow by: "Show me smooth." Now say, "What is this?" and point to either rough or smooth.

Repeat, using the other quality.

Technique

If the child should make a mistake, *do not correct*. Smile, put the work away, and teach it at another time.

Do not talk to the child during a lesson. To be effective, the teacher uses only the words she wishes to teach, leaving discussions for other times during the day. *This is important*. The child cannot concentrate upon the concept being taught if she must listen to words not directly related to that concept.

The child must use only the first two fingers in any of these developmental exercises. Again, you as the teacher must know whether the child is right- or left-handed and must use the preferred hand in all these techniques.

Timing   You should begin with three-year-olds, but any child from three to six who has not had sense training will profit by it, as will the retarded.

Preparatory Lesson B:
Rough and Smooth Boards, Two

Procedure

Take the blue board, number two, to the child's table. Ask him to wash his hands; then sit beside him.

Lay the board on the table with the stripes in a horizontal position. Taking the child's first two fingers in your hand, run them gently from left to right across the top sanded bar of the board, saying "Rough."

Move to the smooth section under the sanded bar. Slide his fingers across it, saying "Smooth." Repeat to the bottom of the board.

Ask the child to repeat the performance without your aid.

Tell him he may use the board when he wishes to do so, and make sure he is aware of its place on the shelf.

Leave him.

Technique

The child's fingers must always move from left to right because the movement forms part of the memory he will need as he begins to read.

Show him how to hold his second and third fingers with his thumb as he strokes the boards.

Timing

Age three upward.

Instructions for Preparing the Materials for Preparatory Lessons A and B

Materials

- P-26a and P-26d* of the Packet for Colored Materials
- sharp scissors
- a ruler
- a container of white glue and a small brush
- a 5½-by-8½-inch piece of thin plywood (two needed)
- a sheet of sandpaper and a small can of good varnish
- a small amount of very fine sand

Preparation

Copy on the prescribed colored paper P-26a and -26d from the packet for colored materials. Cutting carefully, remove the 5½-inch section containing the plate for the rough-smooth board away from both the blue letter *u* and the pink letter *f*.

Prepare the plywood by (a) cutting it to the exact size of the plate; (b) sanding the pieces until they are very smooth, paying strict attention to the condition of the edges; and (c) varnishing it with a good varnish.

When the varnish is thoroughly dry, brush an even coat of white glue on one side of both pieces. Attach the cards that have been cut to fit exactly the 5½-by-8½-inch pieces of plywood. Smooth them firmly to insure a good binding action.

Place them under a stack of books or another heavy object until they are thoroughly dry. When they are dry, remove them.

Place the boards on a piece of newspaper. Using the small brush, put a very even, very thin coat of white glue on the large rectangle of the pink board. Sprinkle the glue with an even coat of the fine sand and let it stand ten minutes. Carefully shake off any excess sand.

Allow the glue to dry twenty-four hours before using the board.

Repeat the process with the blue board, gluing and sanding the five thin rectangles.

Thoroughly dry, the boards are ready for use. Place them in an assigned place on the classroom shelf.

---

*The numerals throughout the text refer to the page numbers on which the materials are illustrated.

Preparatory Lesson C: Fabric Classification, Rough and Smooth

Materials
- a variety of materials whose surface texture is either rough or smooth. (Have twenty different swatches in the box. Velvet, silk, and percale are examples of smooth materials. Hopsacking, tweed, and grosgrain are examples of rough materials.)
- pinking scissors
- a five-by-eight-inch cardboard pattern (a shoebox lid makes one)
- a five-by-eight-inch piece of very fine sandpaper
- a five-by-eight-inch piece of very smooth satin paper
- a blindfold
- a cardboard box, flat, large enough to hold the five-by-eight-inch swatches of fabric

Preparation

Using the cardboard pattern, cut one swatch of each fabric with the pinking scissors and put them into the box. Place the sandpaper and the satin paper on top of the fabrics. Lay the blindfold on top of these. Place the lid on the box and label it *Fabrics 1*. Assign the box to its position on the shelves.

Materials
- a box labeled *Fabrics 1*
- a child's table

Philosophy

The sense of touch must be developed until sight is not needed for identifying differences. The fingertips alone can do this. The materials in this lesson further that development.

Procedure First Lesson

Have the child wash her hands.

Take the box to the child's table. Sitting with her, place the sandpaper and the satin paper on her table—at the top, out of the way. Scramble the rest of the contents of the box on the table in front of her and push the pile to one side.

Pick up one piece of material and smooth it in front of the child. Holding the left edge of the fabric, take the child's hand gently in yours. Run the first two fingers of the child's hand over the surface of the material, touching it very lightly.

Ask if it is rough or smooth. If it is rough, the child begins a stack under the sandpaper; if smooth, under the satin paper. If the child is uncertain, she may again lightly run her fingers from left to right across the sandpaper or the satin paper.

Procedure Second Lesson

After the child has worked successfully with the material and seems to enjoy it, show her the next step.

Ask her to wash her hands.

When she sits with you, show her the blindfold. Place the guides at the top of her table (the sandpaper and the satin paper). Scramble the box contents in the usual manner.

Ask her to put on the blindfold; then have her feel the two guides in the usual manner. Guide her hand to the pile of fabrics. Ask her to choose one and lay it in front of her. Have her hold the left edge firmly as she has been shown. Have her trail her first two fingers lightly over the fabric, determining whether it is rough or smooth.

Have her check the position of the guides; then ask her to flatten under the correct guide the fabrics she has felt.

Have her choose the next swatch and sort it out in the same way. Tell her to proceed through the exercise until all swatches are stacked neatly under the correct guides.

Have her remove her blindfold and check to see if she has done the exercise correctly.

Three years and upward. **Timing**

Preparatory Lesson D:
Fabric Matching

Materials
- another set of fabric scraps, different, if possible, from the previous set in color and texture
- a five-by-eight-inch cardboard pattern
- a blindfold
- pinking scissors
- a cardboard box, large enough to hold swatches

Preparation Using the cardboard pattern, cut two identical pieces of fabric from each scrap. This exercise requires eight pairs of fabrics, differing markedly in surface texture. Wool, velvet, percale, satin, linen, a drapery fabric, velour, and silk make a good variety.

Put the pairs of fabrics into the box, a swatch of every kind in each pile, and place the blindfold on top of the fabrics. Put the lid on the box and label the box *Fabrics 2*. Assign the box its position on the shelves.

Materials
- the box labeled *Fabrics 2*
- a child's table

Philosophy This is a refinement of Lesson C, constructed to further the child's sense of touch. It allows for the growing ability to identify without the use of sight.

Procedure Have the child wash her hands and put on the blindfold.

Join her at her table with the box *Fabrics 2*. Separate the fabric pairs into two random piles, one to the right and one to the left of the child. Select two of the fabrics with a strong textural contrast, such as wool and satin, from the right hand pile. Place them in front of the child and ask her to feel them. She may hold the fabric securely with her free hand, pressing firmly either on the left edge of the swatch so her feeling motion moves from left to right, or on the top of the swatch so her feeling motion moves from the top to the bottom of the swatch. Either way, she lifts her fingers from the material and returns them to the beginning for her next stroke. It is important to her future writing competence that she carries through on this stroke-lift-return, stroke-lift-return motion.

The child selects a swatch from one side and lays it on the table in front of her. She then feels it as she has been shown. The swatch is left in front of the child as she feels for the matching swatch from the opposite side. She may check the swatch she is trying to match at any time.

When she decides on a swatch from the opposite side, show her how to lay it beside the swatch in front of her. Have her feel both pieces of fabric. If she still thinks she has a match, show her how to lay the one piece on top of the other. She can do this neatly by feeling and matching the edges.

When she is satisfied the two are neatly arranged, have her place them out of action at the top of her table. Have her choose another swatch from her right-hand pile, match it with one from the left-hand pile, stack the two neatly, and place them with the other pair at the top of the table, again attempting to make sure all the edges match.

Have her finish the game, matching all the pairs without removing the blindfold. When she is finished, have her remove the blindfold and check her accuracy.

Timing Children three to six. Sometimes seven-year-olds will show an interest in the technique.

Preparatory Lesson E:
The Secret Bag

Materials

- 1 fabric drawstring bag
- a set of things common in the child's environment. These should not be toys, but real objects such as those in the following list: pencil, pen, small screw, large screw, bolt, nut, walnut, small rock, eraser, paper clip, clothes pin, small box, rubber band, teaspoon, fork, key, small bottle, bottle top—at least twenty objects.
- a blindfold

Preparation

Obtain a length of sturdy fabric, such as cambric or denim. The material should be twelve inches wide by thirty-six inches long. Hem the twelve-inch edges by turning two inches to the wrong side. Iron under ¼ inch and stitch it flat. One inch from this seam, sew another line of stitching. This is the beading into which the drawstring will be threaded.

Place right sides of the fabric together. Seam both edges on the wrong side ½ inch from the edge. Turn right side out and thread two eighteen-inch cords through the bottom beading channel of the bag's top.

Hooking the index fingers into each of the strings, pull. One string should pull left, the other, right. This will close the bag. Open it and place all the objects you have chosen into it. Place the bag in a small basket; add the blindfold, and assign it to its place on the shelf.

Materials

- the secret bag
- the blindfold

Philosophy

The child needs confirmation of her ability to identify things she knows by touch alone. This exercise is to assure her of her ability to know and recognize things she touches but does not see.

Procedure

This activity is introduced as a group game. Individual children or children in pairs may participate.

When the children have gathered into a quiet group, show them the basket containing the secret bag and the blindfold. Take each object out of the bag, one at a time. Discuss the object, its name, and its use. When the bag is empty and the children have an idea what the objects are, return the objects to it. Close the bag, leaving a small opening.

Ask for a volunteer to find and name the first object. Seat this child on a small chair facing you. Ask her if she wishes to wear the blindfold. (Some will and some won't. Do not insist. Children who are not yet comfortable with the blindfold can participate by closing their eyes.) Put on the blindfold if she wishes to wear it.

Gently guide her hand into the opening of the bag. Tell her to choose an object, keeping it in the bag as she feels it carefully and naming it before she brings it out for all to see.

You may continue with this child or choose another to feel and name the next article. Articles already named are placed on the table where all the children can see them. The teacher returns the articles to the bag when the game is finished.

Each child must learn how to play the game. The individual player blindfolds herself, chooses an object, names it, puts it on her table, and removes the blindfold to check for accuracy.

The children also learn how to play in teams of two. One child is blindfolded. The other acts as leader. The blindfolded child puts her hand into the bag, chooses an object, names it, removes it and shows it to the leader. The leader puts it aside, and the blindfolded child proceeds to the next object.

Timing From 3½ upward.

Preparatory Lesson F:
Exercises for Pencil Control

Materials
- a figure from one of the baskets prepared for this work
- two pencils of contrasting colors
- a child's table

Philosophy

The child has had experience in learning to control his pencil as he has colored the simplest, one-figure designs. He has progressed from a crude beginning, learning to start on the left side of the figure, to move across the inside of that figure in as straight a line as possible, and to stop at the inside of the line making the right boundary of the figure.

He has worked with these simple figures until he can color in regular parallel lines, moving from the left to the right and from the top to the bottom of these simple figures until they are completely colored.

He is now ready to begin to use color as an element of design, keeping him interested in the process and continuing the development of his pencil control.

Procedure

Take the chosen figure and the two colored pencils to the child's table and sit with him. Using one color, completely fill in one portion of the design. Make certain your lines are closely parallel, filling the section with solid color.

Use the other pencil. Fill in the next section. Continue switching pencils as each section is filled with color.

If the child shows interest, let him start his own design, working at the table with you. He may use any of the new designs; the only rules are that each section must be filled with the alternate color and that the lines are so closely laid as to make the appearance of a solid block of color. All lines must start at the left edge of the section, moving to the right.

Timing

If the child starts with the first figures at age 3, he will be able to accomplish the more complicated designs by 4 or 4½. Any child who doesn't write well profits greatly from these design techniques, no matter what his age.

Instructions for Preparing the Materials for Preparatory Lesson F

Materials
- P-24a to P-24e of the packet for colored materials
- one basket or small box for each 5½-by-5½-inch figure (two of these figures on each page)
- set of colored pencils, many shades of each color
- set of small frozen juice cans (eight)
- tablet of construction paper containing eight basic colors, or a sheet each of construction paper for the eight basic colors
- scissors
- white glue

Preparation

Have a supply of P-24a through P-24e of the pink materials made at a copy factory. (The copy factory will have the machinery to cut the sheets into 5½-by 5½-inch squares. You may cut the sheets on a good paper cutter, but it is much slower.) Put a supply of each figure in its own separate container.

Remove labels from the collection of juice cans.

Cut a strip from each color of the construction paper. This strip must be long enough and wide enough to wrap completely around the juice can, with a half inch to spare.

Spread glue on the spare half-inch and wrap the construction paper around the can, carefully pressing the glued edge on top of the beginning edge.

When the glue has dried, put four or five shades of each color in each coded can. (All shades of green go in the can covered by the green construction paper, and so forth.)

The colored pencil holders and the pencils plus the containers of figures should have adjacent places on the shelves.

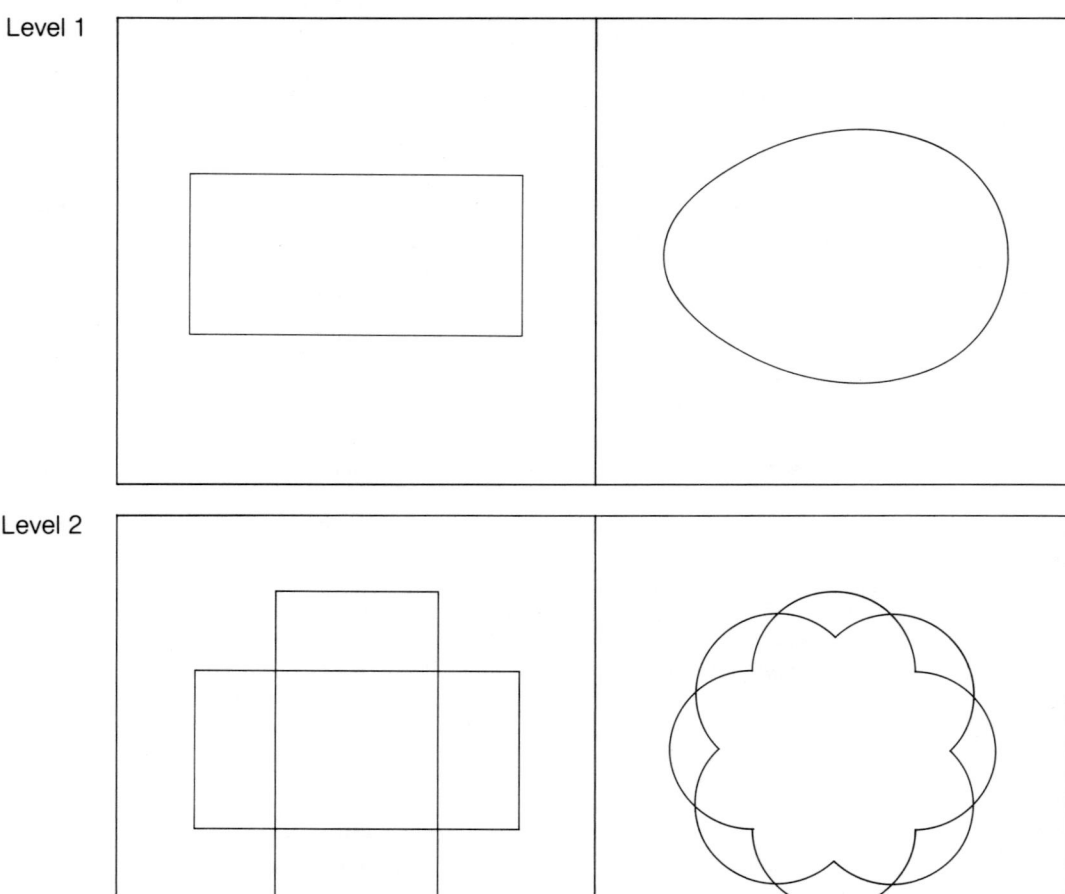

Level 1:
- P-24a   rectangle   ovoid (shown above)
- P-24b   ellipse   circle
- P-24c   quatrefoil   curvilinear triangle
- P-24d   square   equilateral triangle
- P-24e   rhomboid   pentagon

Level 2: P-24f through P-24i (P-24g shown above) are more complicated patterns, using the above figures.

An Introduction to Writing and Reading

A Rationale for Sandpaper Letters

The sandpaper letter forms in the **Pink Reading Lab** manual are designed specifically so that a child need never learn two different methods of handwriting. She need not learn to print vertically, then be taught later to unlearn printing, as children have been required to do for so many years in the belief that such learning assisted in the learning-to-read process. Contrary to the thinking of earlier educators, research has proven early writing need not be based on the circle and stick method of manuscript in order to aid a child's generalization of the printed form to the reading form.

A child quite easily learns the relationship between a clear, cursive form of early writing and the printed symbols of early reading. Since the cursive flow is more natural to her, she will develop a clear and legible writing at once if she is allowed to do so. The letters in the **Pink Reading Lab** manual are structured from the clearest cursive form. The joining strokes she will later need are an integral element of the basic form. In the beginning, the child merely prints the cursive letter with no attempt to join the letters in a cursive flow.

The child's earliest letters will look like this as she perfects the forms:

Later the child will express an interest in cursive writing. She will then be shown how to use the joining strokes to allow her letters to flow together, as follows:

At some time later in her development, her letters will begin to slant. She is then given paper with slanted lines intersecting the horizontal guidelines of her paper. These slanted lines aid in her perception of the uniform spacing of her letters, helping produce a clear and legible cursive handwriting.

No child is to be forced into a uniform production of letter formation but is to be allowed to develop her own unique, clear style of writing. All the children are given the same basic training, however.

P-26a through P-26c are the color-coded blue vowels (see packet section).
P-26d through P-26n are the color-coded pink consonants (see packet section).

The Three-Period Lesson

The *three-period method* of teaching new concepts was originally designed by the noted French physician, Edouard Seguin, in the late eighteenth century. This method of helping children learn new material has yet to be improved upon. Madam Montessori saw the value in this method of teaching and incorporated it into her lessons. The writers are pleased to acknowledge Dr. Seguin's contribution.

First period

The teacher selects two to three examples of any concrete material. In this case, we will use color chips and will teach three colors: red, blue, and yellow. Taking the selected material to a child, the teacher presents it in this manner. Laying one of the selected colors in front of the child she says, "This is _____ (red, blue or yellow)." The child repeats the color name, and the teacher withdraws that color. The procedure is repeated until the three colors have been presented and named.

Second period

In the next step of the lesson you, as the teacher, place all three colors in front of the child and ask her to point to the appropriate color as you name it. Ask these questions: "Can you show me red?" "Can you show me blue?" "Can you show me yellow?" If the child does so without difficulty, mix up the colors and repeat the questions. In the beginning, keep the questions in the same order of sequence to help the child learn the material for the first time. As she progresses and gains assurance, you may ask the questions in any sequence.

The object of the lesson is to give information to the child in a manner that reassures her of her ability to select right answers. Never try to trick or mislead her until she has an unwavering grasp of the concept you are teaching.

Third period

This part of the lesson is for the child who has grasped the first two periods. With the less able child, stop the lesson at the end of the second period and reteach those two periods. Do not rush into the third period until you are certain the child has understood the concepts taught in the first two periods. This is an essential caution to be taken with *all* the material in these lessons.

Remove the materials from the child's view. Select one piece, show it to the child, and ask: "What is this?" If the child gives the correct answer, proceed with the lesson, asking her to name the other pieces of material. If the child gives a wrong answer, accept it cheerfully and stop the lesson. Never tell her she is wrong. Merely stop the lesson and reteach from the beginning at the next opportunity.

Lesson One:
Learning the Sounds
of the Sandpaper Letters

Materials

You will have prepared the letters on the pink and blue cards from the materials packet, P-26a through P-26n.

These letters are to be kept in a box marked *Sandpaper Letters* and kept in a convenient place.

Philosophy

This sandpaper-letter approach to learning allows a child to strengthen the knowledge he has gained through the use of three of his sense organs: sight, sound, and touch. Through the cooperation of the senses, his learning is reinforced. This reinforcement brings about a rapid learning of the code necessary for comprehensive understanding of letter sounds. The child's kinesthetic memory of letter shapes aids him in his later development of writing skills.

Procedure

Present two or three letters of widely differing sounds. (Please refer to the sound-letter chart in this lesson. A good selection consists of *c, s, a*. Do not teach the letter name. If the child knows it, show him that the *sound* of the letter is different from the *name*.

Take the selected letters to the child's table. Sit beside him, with the letters out of his sight. Using the *three-period lesson,* present the letters to him.

Make sure the child uses only his middle and index fingers, the other two held back by his thumb, and that he always moves in the writing direction as he traces the letter.

At the end of each lesson, to identify the sounds he has heard in words, you say, "c." "Can you hear 'c' when I say 'cat'? 'car'? 'cow'? 'duck'? 'truck'? 'milk'? 'locate'? 'because'? 'recall'?" (Have a list of words with the sound in the initial, medial, and ending positions.)

Then say, "Can you think of a word that begins with 'c'?" End every lesson in this manner, always using the new sounds taught.

Points to remember

- The child *must* be taught always to trace the letter in the writing direction.
- He must be taught not to raise his fingers until he has completed the letter.
- He must be taught to cross the *f* and *t* in the proper direction, from left to right.
- He must be taught to dot the *j* and the *i*.
- He may start to learn these sounds when he is 3½.
- Any child of any age who has not learned them will profit from the lessons.

A young child becomes very interested in writing the letters he has learned as he progresses. When he shows an interest, give him unlined paper and let him write the sounds. If he wishes you to dictate these sounds to him, do so. Do not criticize the formation of the letters, but observe him enough to make sure he starts the letters from the left and moves to the right.

He may wish to write sounds on a chalkboard if it is available.

Never insist that a child write his sounds. All children will eventually do so if left alone and will make a much better job of it than if they are coerced.

A Technical Emphasis

Consonants truly have no voiced sound without the assistance of the vowels. (See below for "Phonetic Sounds.") Hence, the sound of the letter *b* has an overriding tendency to become "buh" when one tries to isolate it as an individual sound. This additional sound confuses and slows the reading process in some children. The vowel sound must be eliminated as much as possible when you teach the child the sounds of the consonants in the alphabet. You can accomplish this most easily by sitting very near the child and dropping the voice to a soft whisper as the sound is reproduced. You should practice the technique before attempting to work with the children.

Children 3½ to 4 and any child who cannot read. Timing

Instructions for Preparing the Materials for Lesson One

- sandpaper-letter cards Materials
- a sharp paper cutter
- white glue
- fine-grained sand
- a quarter-inch brush with firmly fixed bristles

The sandpaper letter forms are the first materials in this section of *The Pink Reading* lab manual. Color coding begins here. Of the twenty-six alphabet cards, twenty-one are the pink consonant cards, and five are the blue vowel cards. Sources of materials

White glue may be obtained from any office supply shop, supermarket, or drug store.

Both the fine-grained sand and the small brush may be obtained at a good hobby shop.

Copy onto colored paper the large alphabet cards numbered P-26a through P-26o in the materials packet. Preparation

Using a sharp paper cutter, separate the letter cards, using the guidelines.

Brush white glue sparingly but evenly within the lines of a single letter. Cover the lines precisely. Brush glue on only *one card* at a time. Finish that card before proceeding to the next.

Hold the newly glued card over a paper. Using the first two fingers and the thumb, sprinkle the fine sand upon the wet glue. Do not remove the excess sand until the glue has dried. Set the card aside and proceed to the next.

When the glue has dried thoroughly, tap the card gently to remove excess sand.

Allow the glue to dry for several days before using the letter.

The unchanging sounds of the alphabet are the sounds made by single letters. These are the phonetic sounds and are taught first in this text. Practice saying and hearing the beginning sounds in the following words. Know them thoroughly before you begin teaching the sounds with the sandpaper letters.

Sound-letter chart

a as in *apple*	j as in *jump*	s as in *see*
b as in *boy*	k as in *kite*	t as in *top*
c as in *cat*	l as in *let*	u as in *up*
d as in *dog*	m as in *man*	v as in *very*
e as in *end*	n as in *no*	w as in *will*
f as in *fig*	o as in *on*	x as in *fox*
g as in *girl*	p as in *pig*	y as in *yellow*
h as in *hop*	q as in *quick*	z as in *zoo*
i as in *it*	r as in *run*	

- The teacher must be *precise* in demonstrating tracing letters as the child is taught the sounds of the alphabet. Generally this is from the top of the letter down, then adding any form to the right as needed, or moving from a one o'clock position upward, around, and down to the left, then up or down to complete the letter. Notes of interest
- Correct instruction at this stage will insure proper movement as the child goes into writing beautifully formed letters.
- The child must be taught to use the first two fingers of his hand, keeping his fingers arched, his wrist up. If he cannot do so, his motor coordination probably has not developed sufficiently to allow him to begin working with the material.
- Proper instruction at this stage also helps eliminate much of the early confusion

concerning letters with similar configurations.

Please study and know the instruction chart in the "Introduction to Writing and Reading," "A Rationale for Sandpaper Letters" section of this book that deals with the tracing of the letter forms.

Lesson Two: Using the Coded Alphabet

Materials
- the letters of the movable alphabet, placed in a sectioned box (*All vowels are together. Do not alphabetize the letters.*)
- a three-by-six-foot mat or rug

Philosophy

The child is now introduced to a method of using the material she already knows—the sounds and shapes of the letters of the alphabet. With the teacher's assistance, she now uses an extension of this knowledge in a logical and sequential step. The teacher harnesses the child's natural and spontaneous drive toward ambiguity (moving from the known to the unknown to venture into word formation—an exciting challenge).

Procedure

This is the first instance in which the teacher may use a small group of children. Select three or four of those who know their sounds.

Spread the mat on the floor and place the open alphabet box at the top of the mat.

Ask children to find various letters in the alphabet box as you vocalize the sound of the letters. Continue with the game until all children in the group know the location of each letter in the box. Children who begin to learn the sounds by 3½ should be able to do this step successfully by age 4. Most children will be ready to handle this step two or three months after they begin the sandpaper letters.

Timing

Any child who is four or older.

Instructions for Preparing the Materials for Lesson Two

Materials
- the set of movable letters numbered P-32a through P-32-l in the materials packet
- sharp paper scissors
- a quantity of clear contact paper
- a large sectioned box in which to store the letters

Sources of materials
- Contact paper can be purchased in any good hardware or office supply store.
- A large box can be sectioned off and used for storage of the letters, or a wooden box, especially made for this material, is available.

Preparation

Copy onto colored paper the cards numbered P-32a through P-32-l from the materials packet (these letters are coded pink and blue), and contact each sheet, front and back, with clear contact paper.

Using very sharp scissors, cut out each letter placing all letters of the same sound into one section of the box prepared for the coded alphabet for storage and for use by the child. (Do not attempt to place the letters in the box in alphabetical order. Place the vowels in the first five partitions in a, e, i, o, u order, the others in any random position.)

Vowels, color-coded blue; P-32a through P-32d (in packet section)
Consonants, color-coded pink; P-32e through P-32-l (in packet section)

Lesson Three:
Analysis of Words

Materials

- the coded, movable alphabet
- a three-by-six-foot rug or mat
- not more than two children who know the placement of the letters in the alphabet box.

Philosophy

The natural drive of the child is used to lead him further into the intricate process of code cracking, necessary for fluent reading. The teacher, working with the information the child already has acquired structures and guides his growing ability to analyze words through sound composition. At this point the child must gain the confidence in his ability necessary to extend his knowledge of the process.

Of inestimable value to the child is the teacher's ability to project a quiet and enthusiastic assurance of the youngster's success.

Procedure

Invite one child or two children to join you in the lesson. Together, lay out the large mat and place the movable alphabet at the top of the mat.

You and the child sit around the mat, the child in position to reach the letters in the opened box.

From a list of three-letter, phonetic words you have prepared, pronounce a word, enunciating clearly and carefully in the following manner: "Log. What sounds do you hear when I say log?"

Continue to enunciate very clearly until the child makes the sound of the first letter of the word. Then say, "Yes, 'l.' Can you find 'l'?" The child finds the letter and places it upon the mat.

"What other sound do you hear when I say 'log'?" Very often in the beginning lessons, the final consonant will come next. Accept the sound, positioning it on the mat to leave enough room for a vowel to be fitted into the word. When this happens, point to the empty space and say: "There is a sound that must go here. Listen carefully and see if you can hear which one it is." Then enunciate slowly and clearly until the child hears and produces the missing sound. Now dictate the next word to the child.

Continue this process for the period of time necessary to give the child complete confidence in his ability to form words.

Lesson Four: Objects and Word Building

Materials
- the coded, movable alphabet
- a three-by-six-foot rug or mat
- a pink box of three-letter, phonetic objects

Philosophy

A child moves naturally toward ambiguity. This movement is an intrinsic human process that allows her to put together what she knows, to make generalizations, and to move on to the next higher concept. She does this with joy and enthusiasm when she is not forced to compete with her peers during her early learning.

It is vital that you deal with each child as an individual during this early period. If you do this with care and understanding, the child's own drives are encouraged, and her intrinsic feelings of self-worth are protected. Her self-esteem is never more vital to success and growth than in her early efforts to crack the reading code so that she can learn to read easily and well. She must be given materials that allow her to build upon knowledge she already has integrated and designed to lead her into deeper understanding of the process with which she is involved.

This text is designed to take advantage of what the child knows, to add to that knowledge, and to challenge her to take the next step toward independence. If you use these materials according to plan, each child's success in reading will be gratifying, even when her potential may limit her ultimate ability.

Procedure

Lay the mat on the floor, and place the movable alphabet box in its lid in the upper left-hand corner of the rug.

Open the box of objects, replacing the box in its lid. Take objects from the box, one at a time, allowing the child to name them. This is a test to find out if she is familiar with each object.

Place these objects in a straight vertical row down the left-hand edge of the mat.

Demonstrate the process by saying the name of the first object softly and distinctly to yourself, listening for the individual sounds making up the word. The child will lay the letters she hears beside the object as she discovers each letter of which the word is composed. (Example: *d—o—g.*)

Ignore mistakes in spelling at this time, except if the child leaves the vowel out of one of these three-letter words. If this happens, say quietly: "Did you know every word must have one of the blue sounds in it? Can you hear the sound of the blue letter in *d—o—g*?" (If *dog* happens to be the word she has failed to hear the vowel in.)

The child will begin to listen for the sound needing the blue letter after her attention has been drawn to it in this calm and accepting manner.

Leave the child to work alone as soon as you are sure she understands the process.

Never overteach. Allow the child to use what she knows. Do not demand that the child read the words to you, but listen if she wishes to do so. Read the words for her if she asks you to, but do not do it unless she really invites you to share her work. Do not demand that she write any of these words unless she asks or volunteers to do this.

This work should be understood to be an experience in oral and visual spelling. It *is not reading* and should never be treated as such.

Timing

A child who has learned her sounds will be ready for this work by the time she is four years old.

Instructions for Preparing the Materials for Lesson Four

Materials

- several small boxes, coded pink, size 3-by-3-by-2½ inches (labeled *Set 1*)
- six or eight small objects (taken from the list below) in each box

Objects suitable for lesson boxes:

cub	hog	gum (stick)
bus	cot	rug
cup	tub	fox
dog	nut	mug
box	top	gun
pot	jug	jet (plane)
elk	ant	bug
lad	pig	cat
can	map	elf
wig	rat	bib
fan	man	bat
pin	van	peg
hat	cap	pen
net	lid	bed
bag	kid (young goat)	pan
hen	rag	lid

These objects are miniatures and may be obtained in toy, variety, and hobby shops as well as in the environment. A nut, for example, may be the fruit of a tree or a bit of tooled metal fitting a bolt. Children enjoy learning about both. The list above is a suggested list. By no means take it to be restrictive. Any three-letter, phonic-word object serves the purpose.

Lesson Five:
Noun Game

As soon as a group of children are working through the first boxes of objects and are building words independently, it is time to introduce the concept of the *noun* to the class. The following description concerns the mechanics of this first group game.

The Noun Game

The noun game is used to introduce the idea to the children that a noun is the name of an object.

At some period when the children are through work and are gathered together around you, start the game, playing it in a lively way as if you are joking with the class.

Begin by asking several of the children to bring you things in the room: "Jon, please bring me a book." "Susy, please bring me a pencil."

Do this until the children are happy with the game. Then proceed with the next step, making the request but leaving out the noun. "Jimmy, please bring me a _____." "Please bring me a _____, Jimmy." "Jimmy, why don't you bring me a _____?"

The children will start guessing and will bring all sorts of things to you. Refuse many things, saying "No, thank you. I did not want a block," and so on until at last you accept an article or tell someone to bring something no one has yet thought to bring.

Let the children discover why it was so hard for them to bring the article you wanted. When they know it was because you left out the name of the object you have finally accepted, tell them about nouns being the names of things.

The children will most likely want to repeat this game often. If so, accommodate their desire to do so.

After they have played and enjoyed the game, the children are ready for the introduction of nouns.

This game can begin when the children are 3½. It *must* be played with the four-year-olds who are beginning phonetic work.

Lesson Six:
Writing

Materials

- the chalkboard
- large sheets, twelve-by-eighteen inches, of newsprint, blank
- a supply of sharpened pencils
- chalk
- a chalk eraser

Philosophy

Children who have been led properly through the preparatory lessons at the beginning of this *Pink Reading Lab* manual should voluntarily begin writing the sounds of the letters within six weeks after learning the sounds with the sandpaper letters. Writing usually comes about spontaneously, without strain, and is a natural outgrowth of the development of the tactile sense.

You, the teacher, must always have an available supply of paper on hand for the children to use. And you must be available at any time a child wishes to take dictation. At first, a child will ask you to dictate *sounds* of letters she knows well. As she progresses, she will ask for *words* to write. You must be sure to give her only words containing phonetic sounds as she begins this work.

This desire to write is a natural development in a young child; it needs to be fostered by the alert teacher. Children who do not go through this stage with these materials find writing more difficult later on, both mechanically and creatively.

Procedure

If the child has not come to you by the time she has reached this stage in her progress and asked you to say sounds or words for her to write down, you, as teacher, must show her the materials and introduce her to the fun of writing the sounds she knows.

You may do this either with the chalkboard and chalk or with blank, large newsprint and pencil.

Introduce the child to the material. Pronounce a sound. Ask her to reproduce it. Stay with her as she reproduces several. Tell her to get the sandpaper letters and check to see if she is correct.

Do not correct her.

Leave her at some point in the lesson, telling her she may come to you at any time and you will give her a new sound or a word to write.

Her efforts are not to be criticized or corrected at this time.

The child will write well in three months and almost perfectly in six.

Timing

If a child starts her sandpaper letters at 3½, she will be ready to start writing at four.

Five-year-olds will integrate the skills more quickly. If a child starts the preparatory lessons when she is five, she should be ready in two months to begin the sandpaper letters. When she is finished with those, she will be able to write in a period of four weeks.

Note

The child may use the chalkboard or the unlined newsprint. The teacher should not force her to use either but should only enquire which she would prefer to use.

Note

She may at any time get a sandpaper letter from its box and use it to recall how to shape a letter she cannot remember.

Note

All letters must be formed by the child's own effort. As she practices, she will correct and reshape her own forms. This leads her to a clear and perfect "first" all her own.

Note   The child must be supplied with a vast number of art experiences. Each art experience must be shown to the individual child as structured activity that will provide her an ease of use of the materials. These materials should then be left in an assigned place on the shelf.

The teacher must keep these materials in good order. All components must be available at all times. The child may use any of the techniques she has been shown at any time she so desires.

The sequence in which art activities may be introduced is as follows:

- crayons and paper of varying size
- felt-tipped markers and paper
- beginning watercolor, set at child's table
- clay work
- beginning stitchery
- beginning weaving
- folding (paper and napkins)
- paper punching (making dots) and pasting
- large easel work
- lessons in cutting
- pasting (collage, montage, and similar work)

The opportunity to use these materials whenever they are not in use by some other child is as important as any other work the child does in preparing her hand for the discipline of writing.

Filling in geometric figures with ever-increasing skill is a must for muscular coordination necessary for controlling the pencil. You should sit down periodically and fill in one of these figures, working beautifully and accurately and with evident enjoyment in order to insure a child's continued interest and pleasure in the technique.

The children must be able ultimately to fill in the whole figure with smooth color. No white space should be evident. This work will continue for a very long time as they learn to experiment with the designs they can form.

Lesson Seven:
Nouns, Box 1

■ a box of prepared noun cards, one card for each phonetic-word object in the classroom	**Materials**

Philosophy

The child enjoys the power his knowledge gives him. The evidence that he can use his growing expertise in code cracking gives him impetus and speeds the development of his skill.

Procedure

You may introduce this box as a group game. Take the box into the group of children when they are assembled for a group activity.

Holding the box above a child's head, ask each member of the class to take a card from it and conceal the card from the other class members.

When each child who wants a card has one, ask who would like to be first. That child then sounds out the card to himself and finds the object in the room, placing the card against the object.

Any child unable to read his card is aided by the teacher or a child of his choice as a helper. No child is allowed to fail. A supportive, helping relationship is essential at this stage of learning.

When the children have placed all the cards, ask each one what noun he had to find; then ask him to retrieve the card.

Count all the cards with the children so that they are aware of the number in the box.

Show them how to place the heading card on top of the pile and how to use the rubber band to keep the cards in order.

Place the cards in the box and return it to the assigned place on the shelf, duly noted by all the children.

Materials Management:

Boxes and cards

The teacher will be preparing many boxes and cards, coded as to difficulty and concept. It will pay you dividends in time and material if you mark each box clearly as to function (*Box 1 Nouns* or other appropriate label), and if each card in the box is marked with its box number. All the black cards in noun box one should have a white number one in the lower right hand corner on the back of the card.

Rubber bands

The material will last a greater number of years and will remain in better condition if the teacher, in the beginning, understands the necessity of each child's knowing how to place the cards in a neat stack (with the heading card on top of the stack) and how to fasten the little pack of cards with a rubber band. This technique is absolutely essential to a child's learning. If he is not yet able to hold the cards and place the elastic band around them, help him without question. *Every child must be impressed* with the necessity of replacing the band before returning the material to its box. Keep a supply of rubber bands handy so that any broken band may be replaced without confusion. Any material replaced without the rubber band in position should be noted and removed from the shelf. A group discussion concerning the value of returning all materials to the shelves, ready for the next person's use, is then necessary before you band the loose cards once more and quietly return them to their assigned place. If you do this as soon as the cards are introduced as work material, the children will soon insist upon carrying out your instructions.

Timing

The first noun box should be in the room as soon as several of the four-year-olds know the sounds of the alphabet and are working with the large movable letters.

Months of the year; days of the week   These cards are included in box one and should be used at this time as an awareness material in the classroom. Their use must be casual, with no attempt to teach the names of either the months or the days. For instance, you may mention that a child's birthday is in September, show the card, put it in a special place, and refer to it again and again for that reason or for any other reason. Some children will learn to read these cards as some will learn to read the name of every child in the room. *Do not* teach the names of these cards at this time because deliberate teaching will cause the less able child to believe he is unable to progress.

Preparation   Copy onto colored paper the phonetic nouns from P-40b and P-40d of the pink reading material.

Apply clear contact paper to both sides of the black noun cards.

Using a sharp paper cutter, cut the word cards into 2-by-2½-inch cards, paying strict attention to guidelines.

Place all the three-letter phonetic nouns in one pack of cards, the longer words in another pack. Reserve the pack containing the longer words for later in the child's development.

Contact a heading card from the set of heading cards. This card will say *Nouns*.

Use a rubber band to fasten the pack of noun cards together under the heading card.

A box, color-coded black, should be prepared for these cards. It should be labeled *Nouns Box 1*.

The box should be assigned to a permanent place upon a convenient shelf.

After the children have been shown the cards, they should be allowed to use the box, either individually or with a partner.

Timing   Children four and older will be ready to do this level of work after they have completed the preliminary exercises.

Months of the year: P-40a and P-40b of the materials packet
Days of the week: P-40c of the materials packet
Objects in the room: P-40b and P-40d of the materials packet

Lesson Eight:
Pictured Objects and
the Coded Alphabet

Materials
- a box of pictured objects on pink cards
- the coded alphabet
- a floor mat or a rug

Preparation

Remove cards numbered P-42a through P-42e of the materials packet. Contact both the front and the back of the cards as before. Cut contacted cards into regular size, 2-by-2½ inches. Assemble the cards into boxes of six or eight pictures, using a random selection of middle-vowel sounds.

Warning

Do not give the children sets of pictures that all contain the same vowel sound. Some children are inclined to use the sameness of the central vowel as a crutch. These little ones will become uncertain and uneasy if the vowel sounds are later mixed, and their reading progress will be impeded. It is much better not to give them material allowing them to rely on sameness. They find it quite easy to go ahead without this type of artificial structuring.

Prepare a set of pink boxes large enough to house the selection of cards, six or eight to a box.

Number the boxes and number each set of cards.

Philosophy

This set of material is designed to help children make the transition from the actual object to the more abstract picture. They need this help in order to accept readily that a symbol stands for an object.

Procedure

After inviting a child to participate in the discovery of the new material, spread the mat on the floor, place the coded alphabet box in its lid in the upper left-hand corner of the mat, and sit on the floor with the child. (Once again, this is an individualized lesson.)

Remove the pictures from the box and place them in a neat vertical order down the left side of the mat. Leave enough space between the pictures to prevent the letters spelling the word from touching the letters above or below.

The child identifies the top picture, finds the letters for the sounds, and composes the word. Stay only long enough to be certain she can manage the procedure. Again, make no attempt to force her to read the words aloud.

Be aware of the child's accuracy, and be prepared to reteach the material in a subtle manner that in no way threatens her confidence in her own ability.

Timing

Four years and upward.

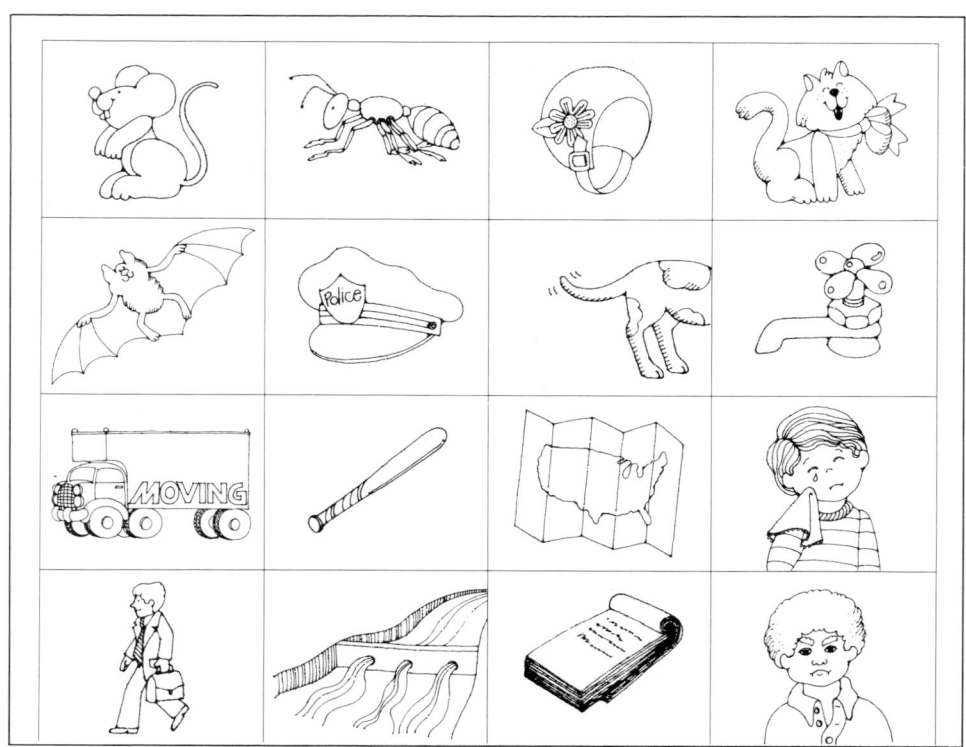

Pictured objects for the color-coded alphabet are numbered P-42a through P-42e in the materials packet. Cut these pictures into 2-by-2½-inch cards.

Lesson Nine: Objects and Word Cards

■ boxes containing six or eight phonetic objects taken from the list in lesson four. (The boxes are colored pink. Have several.) ■ the appropriate 2-by-2½-inch cards from the pink lab manual ■ a child's table ■ a small table mat	Materials
The child is now given material that represents a further abstraction of the concepts he has been working with. This is the beginning of the eye training that will gradually accustom him to the task of reading regular print. In the beginning he is not ready for reading smaller print.	Philosophy
Take a box of objects, pink word cards, and a table mat to the child's table. Spread the mat upon the table and sit with the child. Show him how to lay the objects in a vertical row down the left side of the mat. Hand the child the first card. Listen as he puts the sounds together. As soon as he knows what to do, leave him.	Procedure
Four years and upward.	Timing

Instructions for Preparing the Materials for Lesson Nine

■ several small boxes as for lesson four, color coded pink and numbered *Set 2* ■ from the list in lesson four of this manual, six or eight objects for each box ■ carefully printed, the name of each of the six or eight objects on a label fit into the lid of the box (This label is not necessarily for the child to read, although he may soon do so. It is primarily for your assistance as you make a quick daily check to see that all materials are in order and ready for use.)	Materials
Set one should have labels added to its lids as soon as set two is introduced into the room.	
Copy onto colored paper the word card P-44 in the materials packet. Before contacting, write 9 on the back of each card. Contact the front and back of each uncut pink sheet and cut the cards 2½ inches high. Sort cards according to the objects in the boxes and fasten them with rubber bands. Place the banded cards in their appropriate boxes. Assign the boxes for lesson nine a place on the reading shelf. After the children have been introduced to the material, any child can use any of the boxes in the set.	Preparation

pot	pig	hen	cat
fan	pin	dog	cup
fox	bug	jet	nib
mug	elk	hat	lid

Use P-44, containing three-letter phonetic words, with lesson nine.
Use B-44, containing four-letter phonetic words, with lesson seven.

Lesson Ten:
Large Picture Cards and Word Cards

■ a large card, 8 inches by 10 inches, containing eight pictures of phonetically spelled objects ■ a set of small cards, 2½ inches by 2 inches, containing printed words, three letters in each phonetic word ■ a child's work table	**Materials**

Philosophy

The child, by this time, has gained the information and skills essential for her beginning efforts in reading. She now needs an opportunity to manipulate related materials having the same level of difficulty. Given the opportunity to do so, she can make great gains in her ability to handle and understand new and different-looking tasks. Her reading begins to progress rapidly as she moves through these and the next sets of the phonetic materials coded pink. She gains in spelling awareness and begins the complicated process of abstraction.

Procedure

Take the large card to the child's table.

Remove the envelope from the paper clip. Before beginning the lesson, show the child how to replace the envelope on the back of the large card, using the paper clip. Hold the top edge of the card and the top of the envelope together, the envelope on the back of card. Slide the paper clip down securely over the two edges. This works more efficiently if the long section of the clip slips behind the papers, the short section to the front.

Draw the child's attention to the number on the large card and the number on the envelope. She will understand that sets are kept together.

Lay the large card in front of the child and take the word cards from the envelope. Arrange them in reading order under the large card. Do not make an attempt to have them in the order of the pictures on the card.

Select any card and hand it to the child. Ask her to read it. (Sound it out.)

Ask her to find the picture it is naming, then place the word card under the appropriate picture. Show her how to do it.

As a general rule, do not stay with her after she understands what she is to do. Make sure she knows where the card should be stored, and tell her she may use any of the cards prepared for her whenever she wishes to do so.

Timing

Any child four and older who has shown good progress with the previous materials.

Instructions for Preparing the Materials for Lesson Ten

Materials

■ word cards numbered P-46a, d, g, j, m in the reading material, cut into 2½-by-2-inch cards
■ large cards numbered P-46b, c, e, f, h, i, k, l, n, o in the pink materials packet. (These large cards contain eight line drawings spaced for room under each picture for the appropriate word card.) *Note: These large cards remain uncut.*
■ contact paper
■ rubber bands
■ small envelopes (ten)
■ set of Pentel colored pens if teacher wishes to color the line drawings.
■ paper clips (ten)

Preparation

Copy onto colored paper the section containing the large picture cards and the accompanying word cards from the materials packets.

If the pictures are to be colored, do this now.

Number the back of each large picture card in the lower right-hand corner. Place a corresponding number on the back of each word card.

Work carefully to insure accuracy. Contact all sheets of the set, front and back. Measuring carefully, cut the word cards out, the length to be 2½ inches, the width 2 inches.

Distribute the word cards under the appropriate picture, making sure each picture on the ten large cards has the correct word under it.

Number a small envelope for each of the large cards. Fasten the group of cards for one large card with a rubber band.

Place the cards in the numbered envelope.

Using a paper clip, fasten the envelope containing the words to the back of the card to which it belongs. Do this with all ten sets.

The cards and pictures are now ready to be placed in the room for the children to use.

Note   A standing paper file obtainable from an office supply shop or novelty store makes neat storage for these cards and keeps them in good order as they sit on the shelf.

The large picture cards for this set of materials are to be copied and left intact. They are numbered P-46b, c, e, f, h, i, k, l, n, and o.
The word cards for this set of materials are to be cut into 2-by-2½-inch cards. These cards are numbered P-46a, d, g, j, and m.

Lesson Eleven:
Loose Picture Cards and Words

■ a pink box of materials, containing eight pictures and eight words (These pictured words are three-lettered phonetic nouns as a rule because it is difficult to picture verbs.) ■ a child's work table	**Materials**
This step enhances the child's growing ability toward abstraction. The next step in his development has to do with free association, symbol to symbol. The picture is a symbol of an object; the word is a further abstraction of symbol to object. This material aids the child's development, his ability to leave the concrete and move toward the abstract.	**Philosophy**
Take the box to the child's area, inviting him to join you. Sitting with him, show him how to open the box, placing it in its lid. (It is important to his growing sense of orderliness that he be specifically shown correct care of each new material.) Remove the rubber band from the pack of cards and place it in the box for safe keeping. Lay the pictures in a horizontal row across the top of the table. Hand the stack of word cards, randomly mixed, to the child. Let him choose a card and ask him to sound out the word on the card. Ask him to place it under the related picture. Proceed to the next card. When the child is working well, make sure he knows the place of the material on the shelf and tell him he may use any box in the same manner; then leave him.	**Procedure**
When the child is working well with the large cards and the loose name cards, he may begin this level.	**Timing**

Instructions for Preparing the Materials for Lesson Eleven

■ word and picture cards numbered P-48a through P-48d in the pink materials packet (These are spaced to be cut into 2½-by-2-inch sections. Using a ruler, lightly pencil in the lines to be used as guidelines for cutting these cards.) ■ contact paper ■ rubber bands ■ four boxes, color-coded pink (These should be large enough to store cards without causing them to stick or bind. The boxes must have covers.) ■ a set of Pentel colored pens if you wish to color the pictures before contacting them. (*Caution:* Many colored inks run when the paper stock is contacted. Pentel inks do not. Other brands may not. It is not necessary to color the pictures, but one may do so if one wishes.)	**Materials**
Copy P-48a through P-48d of the materials packet. If the pictures are to be colored, do that now. Lightly pencil in guide lines, dividing the sheet into sixteen cards, 2½ inches long by 2 inches high. A picture or a word will be centered on each correctly divided card. Contact the uncut sheets, front and back. Following guide lines, cut each sheet into 2½-by-2-inch cards. (Each pink sheet of matching word and picture cards make up material for one pink box. These sheets contain enough material for four boxes.) Stack together eight pictures with corresponding word cards and fasten them	**Preparation**

with a rubber band. Place them in a pink box. Remember to number the boxes on the bottom and place a corresponding number on the back of each card in that box.

Each set of this kind of material must be stored in its own separate small pink box.

Have material in its assigned place on the shelf the morning you plan to introduce it.

After a child is introduced to the materials, he is free to use any box he chooses.

(bug picture)	bug	(fan picture)	fan
(kid picture)	kid	(gum picture)	gum
(log picture)	log	(pan picture)	pan
(cap picture)	cap	(rug picture)	rug

This is the material for lesson eleven.
This section is called the Loose Picture Cards and Word Cards.
These cards are all cut into 2-by-2½-inch sections.
They are P-48a, b, c, and d.

Exercises for Pencil Control

Note Please refer to preparatory lesson F in the pink reading lab. Prepare for these lessons in exactly the same manner.

Philosophy The child now must be given the opportunity to increase his growing expertise at pencil control. The simple geometric forms they have been dealing with are now given them in designs that are made by turning the geometric form upon itself 90° to 180°.

Using colored pencils, the children can now begin to produce varied and interesting designs.

Procedure Taking a chosen figure and a variety of colored pencils to the child's table, sit with him and offer him a design. You must sit with him and fill in your own chosen design. The child works along with you, completing his design. The strokes are parallel, each section of the design filled with smooth strokes starting at the top line and continuing straight to the bottom line of the section. The first line is laid in at the far right of the section, the pencil progressing smoothly, top to bottom, right to left, until that section is completely filled with smooth color.

P-24f through P-24h are more complicated patterns of geometric shapes. These are to be used with this lesson and with future lessons.

An Introduction to Grammar

Lesson Twelve:
Farm 1 Nouns

Materials
- the *Farm* box, labeled Farm 1, containing one each of all animals with a phonetic spelling and a packet of noun cards, one card for each object, name printed on the cards, one to each card
- a child's table, or a table designated as the table for this work

Philosophy

The child now needs to use her knowledge of the sounds in different combinations that have definite meanings. It is essential that she begin to learn grammar as she begins to read.

The concept of *noun* at this time is easily assimilated and stimulates a child's natural interest in the function of words. Take advantage of her natural interest by supplying her with materials that fulfill her need to know. Her confidence in herself will grow as the learning process is enhanced

Procedure

Invite the child who is doing well with the loose cards and pictures to come to the "farm table," if you have room for one in the classroom. Otherwise, take the box for Farm 1 to the child's table.

Remove the top from the box, place the lid under it, and place it in an upper corner of her table.

Remove the packet of noun cards from the box and call the child's attention to the heading card that says *Noun*.

Taking a card from the pack, lay it on the table in front of the child and ask her to sound out the word. When she does so, ask her to find the appropriate object (animal).

When she takes the animal from the box, show her how to place it at the top of the card she has just read.

Stay with her until she knows the process, then allow her to work on her own.

After she has been shown this work, the child may use it whenever she wishes to do so.

Timing

From age 4½ upward. Any age child who has no knowledge of grammar will profit from this exercise and from all the following work with grammar.

Instructions for Preparing the Materials for Lesson Twelve

Materials
- a set of black noun cards, P-50c in the pink materials packet
- contact paper
- a set of small farm animals with phonetic names
- the heading card *Noun* from materials packet P-87a
- sharp scissors
- a rubber band
- a box at least 8-by-5-by-2½ inches, preferably plastic, labeled *Farm 1*

Preparation

Copy P-50c from the materials packet.
Contact uncut sheets, front and back.
Cut one label from P-50a and contact it.
Cut the black noun cards into 2½-by-2-inch sections. Rubber band the stack of cards, placing the heading card *Noun* on top.
Add it to the set of animals in the *Farm* box.

noun	noun	noun	noun
verb	verb	verb	verb
verb	article	article	adjective
adjective	verb	singular	plural

These are heading cards, to be prepared and used according to instruction. They are sheets P-50a and P-50b in the materials packet.

pen	hen	bag	egg
cat	man	mom	Nan
dog	fox	dad	kid
ram	mud	hog	pig

Use P-50 for lesson twelve in the pink lab manual and for lesson one in the blue lab manual.
Use B-50 for lesson one in the blue lab manual.

Lesson Thirteen:
Verbs, Box 1

■ the red Verb Box 1	**Materials**

Philosophy

The child has a beginning knowledge that some words are *nouns* and are symbols for persons, places, things, and ideas. It is essential that words that stand for abstractions be given the child as soon as he can understand them, in order that he might receive an early impression of the expanding possibilities of language. A child taught in this way does not have to be drilled in comprehension as he learns to read. Instead, comprehension is his, received with pleasure, as his reading vocabulary increases.

Procedure

This exercise can be introduced as a small group game only to children who are approaching reading. It can also be used as a large group game with all the children in the room who wish to participate, whether or not they are yet able to distinguish words. If children who are not yet sure of their words or their sounds join the group, be sure that an easy, helping atmosphere is maintained. Children who are able may help the uncertain student, or you as the teacher must volunteer your help cheerfully. It is your duty to give help to any child who needs it, cheerfully and without question, in any of these beginning reading sessions.

Gather the children around you and explain that these are *verbs*—words that tell us how to act. Taking the cards from the small box, hand them out, one by one, to the children, or put them into a larger container and mix them thoroughly. Allow each child to pick out his own card from the container you hold out of sight above his head.

Caution the children not to let others see their cards unless they wish to be helped with the sounds. Give each child a turn to read his card silently. Then ask him to place the card face down in front of him. Ask him to stand and silently carry out the action called for upon the card, such as "hop." The other children guess the word on the child's card from the action.

This becomes a favorite game with the children. After they have been through it several times, show them the extension of the game, played by two or three children, as follows.

Extension of Lesson Thirteen: Acting Out the Verbs

■ the red Verb Box 1
■ a floor mat or a rug

Materials

Procedure

Invite two or three children who can read the verbs to join you.

Unroll a mat or a rug on the floor and have the children sit around the rug.

Open the verb box, taking off the rubber band and the heading card and placing them in the lid of the box. Take the verb cards from the box and turn them upside down; then put them back into the box.

Invite one of the children to begin by taking the first card off the pack and performing the action. Let the rest of the group guess what the action is. When someone guesses correctly, the actor shows the card, and the one with the correct answer gets to choose the next card and do the action. The actor returns the card to the lid of the box.

Continue the game until all the cards have been returned to the box lid. They may then be shuffled, and the game may be continued if the children wish to do so.

Variation	The children may elect to have the action progress from one to another in an orderly manner around the rug.		
Variation	Two children may play, one child acting out from all the cards, the other child guessing. When the cards are shuffled, the children reverse roles.		
Variation	Any child may elect to enact the verbs entirely on his own, reading the cards and performing the action for his own benefit.		
Timing	From age 4½ to 6½ or for any child who does not understand the function of verbs.		
Extension	Add B-52 of the materials packet to keep the child's interest alive as his skill grows.		

Instructions for Preparing the Materials for Lesson Thirteen

Materials
- the set of red verb cards P-52 and B-52 in the materials packet
- contact paper
- the heading card *Verb* from the materials packet P-50a
- a ruler and a pencil
- sharp scissors
- a rubber band
- a small box, color-coded red, to contain the 2½-by-2-inch verb cards

Preparation
Copy onto red paper P-52 and B-52 from the materials packet.
Lightly pencil in the lines dividing the sheets into 2½-by-2-inch cards. The lines should be drawn so that the words are in the center of the cards.
Contact the uncut sheets, front and back.
Contact the heading card *Verb*.
Cut the red verb cards into 2½-by-2-inch sections.
Add the heading card to the stack, encircle the stack with a rubber band, place the stack in the box, and label it Verbs 1.

nag	fan	mad	run
tap	gag	rap	yap
beg	pet	dig	sit
hit	jig	sip	nod

Use P-52 with lesson thirteen.
Use B-52 with the extension of lesson thirteen.

Lesson Fourteen:
Confusing Words

Materials
- a yellow box of confusing words
- a child's table

Philosophy

Some words in the English language have no apparent reason for the particular sounds they stand for. Many of these words occur in the first few months of the child's beginning reading experience. She must be given some method of handling these misfits in the orderly pattern she is learning. A critical rule in this method of teaching reading is that a child never be forced to confront anything that will confound her developing reading expertise. Give these first few words to the child in a manner that is both nonthreatening and helpful. She may learn them quickly, or she may take her time. You must see to it that her opportunities to practice them are regular enough to insure her success when she is ready to begin reading in a month or six weeks. This phase of the reading method *must be* taken care of at this time.

Procedure

Take the box to the child's table. Choosing two or three of the cards, teach her the words with the *three-period lesson*. Do this daily until she has mastered the words. Review occasionally.

Timing

This phase should be done with children who can perform the extension of lesson thirteen: "Acting Out the Verbs."

Instructions for Preparing the Materials for Lesson Fourteen

Materials
- the yellow page P-54a of the packet
- a ruler and pencil
- contact paper
- 2½-by-5½-by-1-inch yellow box
- a small spray can of yellow enamel if no yellow box is available
- scissors
- a rubber band

Preparation

Mark guidelines so that each word is centered in a two-by-five-inch strip.
Copy the sheet onto yellow paper.
Contact the yellow sheet, uncut, both front and back.
Cut the sheet into cards two inches wide by five inches long.
Stack the cards and fasten with the rubber band.
Place them in the yellow box.
Assign the box to its position on the shelf.

I	this
the	that
are	they
is	was

The child at this reading level needs to know the confusing words on the following three sheets. Starting with those on P-54a, teach them as puzzle words by the method of the three-period lesson. Add sheets B-54b and B-54c gradually as new games.

Lesson Fifteen:
Farm 1 Adjectives

Preparatory Exercise

During a group meeting, introduce the concept of *adjective* to the children by playing a game similar to the game that introduced the concept of *noun*.

Ask the children in the group to bring you one of several similar objects in the room, using one or more adjectives to describe it accurately: "John, bring me a small, pink flower, please." "Sue, please bring me a large, red flower."

The next step is, without using adjectives, to have the children bring you a number of things: "John, please bring me a book." As the objects are brought, refuse several, such as a blue book, a red book, and a large book. Finally say something like this: "Oh, thank you Jim. I wanted the small yellow book."

Play this game for quite some time. The children will become alerted to grammar usage and will usually spot the difficulty and make the generalization without aid from the teacher.

As soon as the children recognize that you are not describing the article you desire, give them a definition of *adjective* as a word that *describes* a *noun*.

Note

A and *the* are indefinite and definite articles. They are not brought to the attention of the child at this time. The articles are simply introduced as adjectives, which they are.

Materials

the Farm Box, containing objects, noun cards, and adjectives

Philosophy

The child needs to expand her use of the techniques she has learned in an interest-arousing, ongoing manner. This beginning experience with grammar on a level she can readily handle insures an easy, happy attitude toward one of the really neglected areas of education.

Procedure

Take the Farm Box to the table of any child who has enjoyed setting out nouns.

Tell her she is ready to learn to use adjectives.

Have her set out the farm objects and the noun cards for each. Help her if she wishes to have you do so.

Take the light blue cards and explain that these are special adjectives.

Place the light blue card to the left of each of the noun cards, having the child read the resulting phrase aloud.

Now take the first dark blue adjective off its pile. Have the child read it. Perhaps it is "big." Ask, "What farm object could be big?" Suggest some answers, such as, "A big man," "A big dog," "A big bull." When she decides where she wishes to place the card, let her do so.

Have her read the phrase. In the beginning, a child will often put the card in the wrong position. Your reading the words in their order will help her understand the necessity of putting the card in the correct sequence: "strong a big bull," or "a bull big." These combinations of words will not sound right to her.

She goes through all the adjective cards, sounding them out, and placing them in correct sequential order.

Note

The child who is writing will wish to record her phrases. Provide her with the materials she needs to do so.

Timing

Children from 4½ upward enjoy this work.

Extension

Add B-56a of the materials packet to keep the child's interest alive as her skill grows.

Instructions for Preparing the Materials for Lesson Fifteen

Materials
- a set of light blue and dark blue adjective cards from the materials packet, P-56 a, b, and c
- contact paper
- two heading cards: *Adjective* from P-87b
- a ruler
- a pencil
- sharp scissors
- two rubber bands

Preparation Copy P-56a, b, and c onto light blue and dark blue paper as indicated.
Lightly pencil in the lines dividing the card into 2½-by-2-inch sections. Arrange the lines so that the words are in the center of the cards.
Contact the uncut sheets.
Cut the adjective cards into 2½-by-2-inch sections.
Contact and cut the heading cards.
Divide the adjective cards into light blue and dark blue stacks.
Add the heading cards to the top of each stack.
Encircle each stack with a rubber band.
Add the cards to the Farm Box.

a	a	a	a
a	a	a	a
a	a	a	a
a	a	the	the

Use P-56a, b, and c with lesson fifteen.
Use B-56a with the lesson extension of lesson fifteen, as the child's skill dictates.

Lesson Sixteen:
Pink Word Lists

one pink Word List	**Materials**

Philosophy

The child is now supplied with a new material that allows him to confirm his knowledge. He is given practice in an interesting, nonthreatening way.

He begins to experience a great deal of satisfaction in his ability to apply his skills to new materials and to handle each new material with ease.

Procedure

Take one of the word lists to the child's table and ask him to read the list. Make sure he knows that there are many more lists available for him to use.

Allow him to set his own pace.

Timing

From age 4½ upward.

Instructions for Preparing the Materials for Lesson Sixteen

Materials

- long pink cards numbered P-58a, b, c, d, and e of the materials packet.
- a paper punch
- ten eighteen-inch lengths of pink wool yarn
- contact paper
- scissors

Preparation

Copy the section containing the pink word lists in the materials packet.
Copy the page onto pink paper.
Contact the uncut sheets, front and back.
Using the paper punch, punch a hole one inch from each edge of the pink card and a half inch from the top. Do this with all the cards.
Thread an eighteen-inch length of pink yarn through the hole punched at the top of each card and tie the ends into a neat bow.
Hang the cards on hooks prepared for them in the classroom, two or three bunches to each hook.

tap	bad
let	yes
pip	vim
ox	cod
sum	hum
ham	had
get	hem
bib	big
dot	bog
dug	sip

These materials, for lesson sixteen, are P-58a through P-58e.

Lesson Seventeen: Nouns, Singular and Plural

Materials
- the black box marked *Nouns, Singular and Plural, Rule 1*
- a child's table or a rug on the floor

Philosophy

Again the child is given new and interesting material that allows her to use her growing knowledge in a useful and productive manner. This material helps satisfy her curiosity about words and their meanings and how those meanings are changed. She is doing work that means something, that leads her into new generalizations.

Her interest in the ambiguity of the world is fed, forcing her gently into new and greater exploration at the same time that her confidence in her ability is growing.

She is given a systematic way of studying the formation of noun plurals in English.

Procedure

All of these nouns will be of the easy-to-read kind. Some of the objects named in the cards may be things found in the classroom and need not be included in the objects in the noun box.

The child finds the objects in the room, perhaps a flag or flags, and brings them to her work area.

Show her how to take the packets of cards from the boxes. The boxes should sit in the lids, the singular-noun box to the left of the work area, the plural-noun box to the right.

Show her how to lay out the heading cards:

singular   *plural*

Present a three-period lesson, making sure the child can read the heading cards.

Have the child take a card from the singular pile, read it, and lay it under the *singular* heading card. Then have her fetch the object and lay it to the right of the noun card.

Ask her to look in the plural pile for the card naming the same object and lay it under the plural heading, then put several objects of the kind named to the right of the black noun card.

Her work will look like this:

singular	plural
pin	pins
clip	clips
button	buttons

In this exercise, be sure the child does not get the mistaken idea that two is the only plural. She must realize "plural" can and does mean any number more than one. She should be encouraged to put various quantities alongside the plural cards naming the objects.

Timing   Age 4½ and upward, or any child who has no real understanding of the function of words.

Instructions for Preparing Materials for Lesson Seventeen

Materials
- a set of black noun cards, P-61
- contact paper
- sharp scissors
- a ruler and a pencil
- two boxes, each three-by-three-by-one inch, and a larger box about four-by-six-by-three inches
- heading cards, P-50b, one labeled *singular,* one *plural*
- two rubber bands
- a small can of black spray enamel

Preparation   Copy the pages from the materials packet on their designated colored sheets.

Using the ruler, lightly pencil in the cutting lines for 2½-by-2-inch cards—the words to be positioned in the center of each card.

Contact the front and back of the uncut sheet and cut out the cards.

Stack the singular nouns in one pile, the plural nouns in another.

Contact the cards reading *singular* and *plural* and place them on the proper piles.

Fasten them with a rubber band.

Spray the boxes black and let them dry thoroughly.

Copy and cut two more heading cards (*singular* and *plural*) from P-50b. Glue these two cards to the lids of the small black boxes.

Put the cards headed *singular* in their box, those headed *plural* in the plural box.

Gather up the objects named on the noun cards and put a single object for each of the nouns in the singular box.

Place the lid in position and place the box into the larger box.

Place at least two, but preferably many, of the objects named into the plural box and place it into the larger box.

On the lid of the larger box write

Nouns,
Singular and Plural, Rule 1

Assign the box to its position on the shelf.

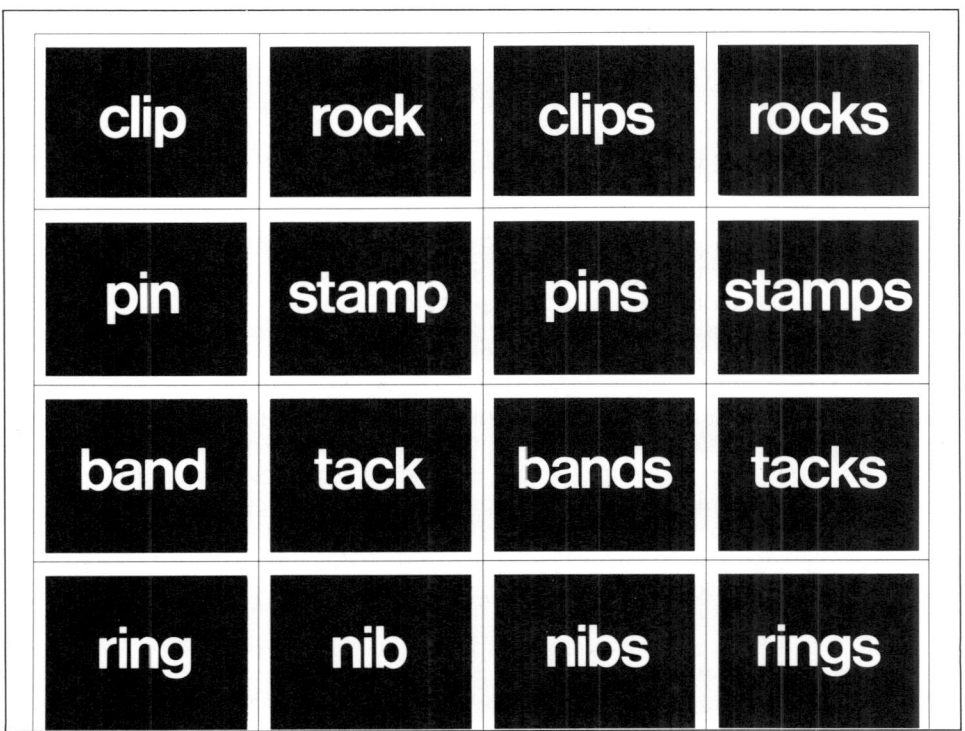

This is the card for lesson seventeen.

Lesson Eighteen: Farm One Verbs

Materials
- the Farm Box 1, now containing a set of farm animals, noun cards naming the animals, two sets of adjectives, and verb cards.
- a child's work area or a special table for work with the farm project box

Philosophy By this time the child should have practiced with the first box of verb command cards enough so that he has a fair idea of the function of the red verb card. The ideas that a verb tells what a noun *does,* that a noun exists, and that a noun is acted upon are beginning to take shape in the child's consciousness. He cannot yet express this knowledge of the function of a verb, but his *experiencing* the function helps him to clarify the verb concept and to make the knowledge his own. Adding verbs to the farm project at this time helps the child as he begins to form sentences with real meaning.

Procedure Again, the teacher presents the work to the individual child who has shown a lot of interest in verb commands.

When the child is ready, place the verb cards in the Farm 1 box and invite him to join you in the new work.

Show the child how to form sentences, and repeat the process until he grasps the meaning of the work.

Play a game of rearranging his sentences to make no sense and ask the child if he can put the sentences back into sensible form.

Note Those children who are interested in writing may wish to copy the sentences they have made. Supply pencils in the four colors they will need to do this.

Point out that all sentences begin with a capital letter and end with a period.
Help the children who are interested form the capitals they need.
Put up a chart of capital letters in the room if the children seem interested.
Help with placing periods.
Do not correct letter shapes.

Extension Add verbs from B-63a through d as the child's skill increases to keep his interest high.

Timing Age 4½ and upward.

Instructions for Preparing Materials for Lesson Eighteen

Materials
- a set of red verb cards, P-63a, b, and c from the materials packet
- a ruler and a pencil
- sharp scissors or a paper cutter
- contact paper
- heading card *Verbs* from P-50b
- a rubber band

Preparation Copy verb card pages onto red paper.

Draw light lines dividing the sheets into 2½-by-2-inch cards. The words should be centered on the cards.

Contact the uncut sheets front and back and cut the sheets into cards.
Contact and cut the heading card *Verbs*. Place it on top of the packet of verbs.
Fasten the stack with a rubber band and add it to the Farm 1 box.

ran	sat	mop	was
run	fed	is	not
sit	tug	is	not
hop	cut	is	not

Materials for lesson eighteen: P-63a, b, and c.
Use B-63a, b, c, and d as child's skill increases.

Lesson Nineteen: Definite and Indefinite Articles

Part One

Materials
- Box 1, *Definite* and *Indefinite Articles*
- cards from materials packet, P-65

Philosophy This is a lesson in the subtlety of the use of the article in the English language. This knowledge becomes an aid in composition and spelling.

Procedure The child sorts the objects into groups, placing all similar objects together in a vertical line.

Say to the child, "When there is only one object, we say 'the' (object)." The child now places *the* in front of each *single* object.

Now take one single object from one of the groups. Say to the child, "When the object is one of many, we call it 'a' (object)." (a nut.)

The child now takes all the rest of the objects in the group and places an *a* in front of each one. She continues with the work until every *a* is used.

She must now be able to practice the lesson whenever she desires until she masters the technique.

Part Two

Materials Box 2, *Definite* and *Indefinite Articles*

Procedure Take the material to the child's table.

Remove heading cards and place them at the top of the child's table.

    Article   *Noun*

Sort the noun cards into their proper categories. Place each series of nouns in a vertical line under *Noun* heading card.

Sort the article cards, placing them in their proper positions.

Instructions for Preparing the Materials for Lesson Nineteen

Materials
- two boxes, same size, colored blue, large enough to hold the variety of articles needed for lessons one and two (These articles must be supplied in exact amounts, one set required):
   - 3 miniature cans (Photo film cans are excellent.)
   - 1 small plastic fox
   - 2 costume jewelry rings
   - 1 small plastic bug
   - 2 small plastic lads (boys)
   - 3 safety pins, diaper size
   - 2 nuts from tool chest
   - 2 nuts from nut tree
- a set of article cards (P-56d) from materials packet (fourteen of *a*, two of *the*)
- two each, *Article* and *Noun* heading cards from P-50b
- contact paper

Preparation Contact and cut out all cards (copied onto blue paper).
Label boxes *Box 1* and *Box 2, Definite* and *Indefinite Articles*.
Place the objects listed above, in exact amounts, in the set.

Sort out fourteen of *a* and two of *the*. Head them with a card saying *Article* and fasten the cards with a rubber band.

Place this set of cards in Box 1, Definite and Indefinite Articles.

Now prepare Box 2 by contacting and cutting out the cards as before.

Place the heading cards on their proper stacks and fasten them with rubber bands.

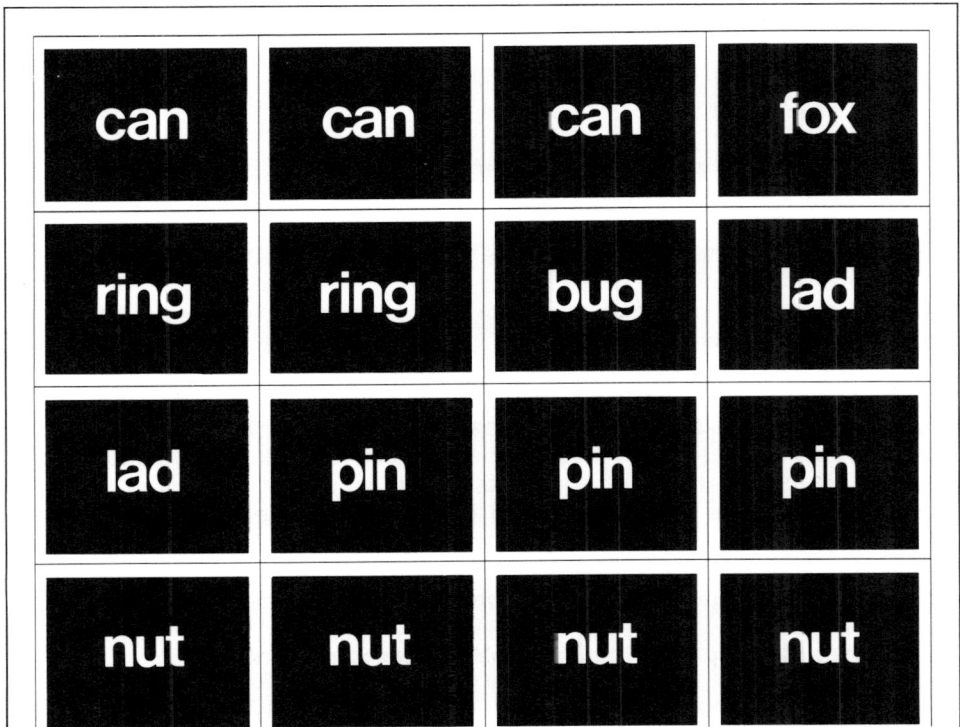

These materials, P-65, are for lesson nineteen.

Lesson Twenty:
Secret Words

Materials	■ the Secret Box ■ a child's work area
Philosophy	The child is beginning to feel the power of his ability. This material is designed to further test that ability in a way that will neither cause him to withdraw nor to fail. He needs much assurance at the same time that he needs to feel himself making real advancement. Any child who has progressed this far knows he is able and shows a definite interest in his own ability.
Procedure	Take the first box to the child. Make sure he knows there are other boxes. Show him how to place the empty lid beside the full box. Have him remove the first slip from the box, unfold it, and read it. (He may read silently or aloud, as he chooses. He may read it to someone or to himself.) Have him refold the slip, place it in the lid, and take another slip from the box. He may do this whenever he wishes to do so.
Timing	From age 4½, or any child who has completed much of the foregoing work.

Instructions for Preparing the Materials for Lesson Twenty

Materials	■ a set of pink word sheets (P-67a, b, c, d, e, f, g, h, i, and j) ■ a ruler and a pencil ■ five boxes, suggested size 3½-by-3½-by-2 inches ■ scissors or a paper cutter
Preparation	If the boxes are not pink, spray them with a good pink enamel. Set them to dry. With the ruler and the pencil, divide each pink sheet of four words into equal-sided squares, centering the words in the middle of each square. Cut out the squares. Fold each resulting slip in half, then the long way. This will result in a small folded square. Put eight of these folded slips into each of the pink boxes. Label each box top *Secret Words*. Assemble them in an assigned place on the shelf.

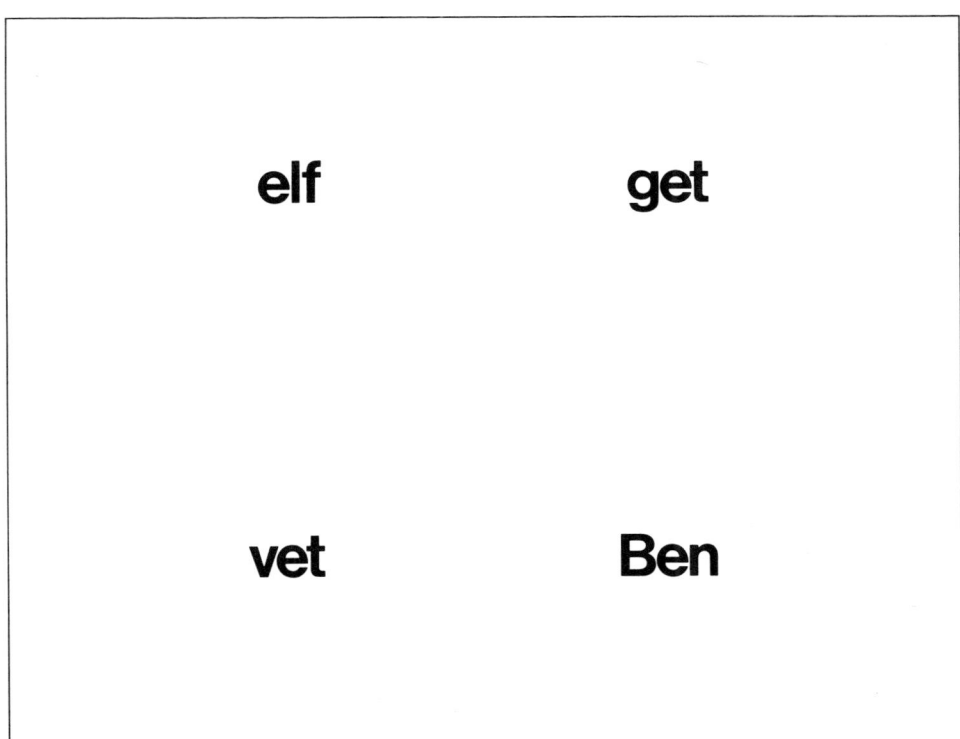

Use P-67a through P-67j with lesson twenty.

Lesson Twenty-One: Verbs, Box 2

Materials the box of *Verb Commands, Set 2,* either A or B of the material

Philosophy The challenge now for the child is to take several words, read them, interpret their meaning, and translate the meaning into action that others can define.

The child who is ready has a consuming drive to see if she can do this. Her need fires her ability to act out the command she reads.

Children can gain amazing interpretative skills from this exercise.

Procedure Choose two or three children who will have no difficulty with the words. Assemble them into a group, showing them the box of commands.

Allow the first volunteer to extract a card. While others watch, ask her to act out the command printed on the card—often to go and obtain a prop from somewhere in the room.

The group waits quietly while she gets ready and carries out the action.

The group tries to guess the exact words written on the card from viewing the action. The child acting the command may repeat the action if those watching are not able to guess what the card says.

When the action is guessed correctly, the actor reads the command aloud and returns the card to the empty lid of the box.

The next child then volunteers to be the actor, and the game continues until all the commands have been drawn from the box.

Timing Age 4½ upward.

Variation A child may choose a box and do the actions for a friend.

Variation Two children may take turns acting out the verb commands for each other.

Instructions for Preparing the Materials for Lesson Twenty-One

Materials
- the red verb command cards, P-69a, b, c, d, e, and f
- two boxes, at least 2½-by-5½-by-1 inch
- a can of red enamel spray
- a ruler and a pencil
- scissors
- rubber bands
- contact paper

Preparation If red boxes cannot be procured, obtain white ones and spray them with red enamel. Set them aside to dry.

Copy onto red sheets the pages containing the verb commands. Using the ruler, center the sentences within guidelines, making each card exactly two-by-five inches.

Contact the uncut sheets, front and back, and, following the guidelines, cut out the cards.

Write *Commands, Set 2, A* and *Commands, Set 2, B* on two cards; glue them to the tops of the two boxes.

Divide the command cards into equal sets and fasten each set with a rubber band.

Store the two sets in the prepared boxes in assigned spots on shelves.

Pick up a pin.	**Hang a hat.**
Stand and hop.	**Sit and hum.**

Material for lesson twenty-one; P-69a, b, c, d, e, and f.

Lesson Twenty-Two: Sentences and Pictures

Materials	- one of the pink sentence-strip boxes - a child's work area
Philosophy	The child should now be able to put his knowledge and skill together and take a firm first step toward reading interpretatively. This material is the first test of that ability.
Procedure	Take a box to the child's work table and sit beside him. Set the box in its lid and remove the box's contents. Stack the pictures to the child's left and shuffle the sentence cards. Place one on the table in front of the child. Sweep your hand from left to right under the words; then remove your hand. Ask the child to read the strip, making sure (very quietly) that he starts the reading with the left-hand word. When he comes to the period, stop. Explain what the period is and what it does. Explain that he is to read the strip without stopping between words. He needs now to realize he must always read straight through to the end of each sentence.
Timing	Age 4½ upward.

Instructions for Preparing the Materials for Lesson Twenty-Two

Materials	- pink cards from P-71a, b, and c - Pentel coloring pens - a ruler and a pencil - contact paper - four boxes, 8½-by-2½-by-1 inch, colored pink - a small can of pink spray enamel - four rubber bands - scissors
Preparation	If pink boxes cannot be procured, obtain white ones and spray them with pink enamel. Set them aside to dry. If you wish to color the pictures, do so now. With the ruler and the pencil, divide the sentences on the pink cards into strips 7½ inches long by 2 inches wide. Divide the accompanying pictures into 2½-by-2-inch sections. Contact the uncut sheets, front and back and cut them into the sentences with their matching pictures. Fasten the pictures on the top of the correct sentence strips and place them in their boxes. Assign the boxes to an area on a shelf.
Timing	Age 4½ upward.

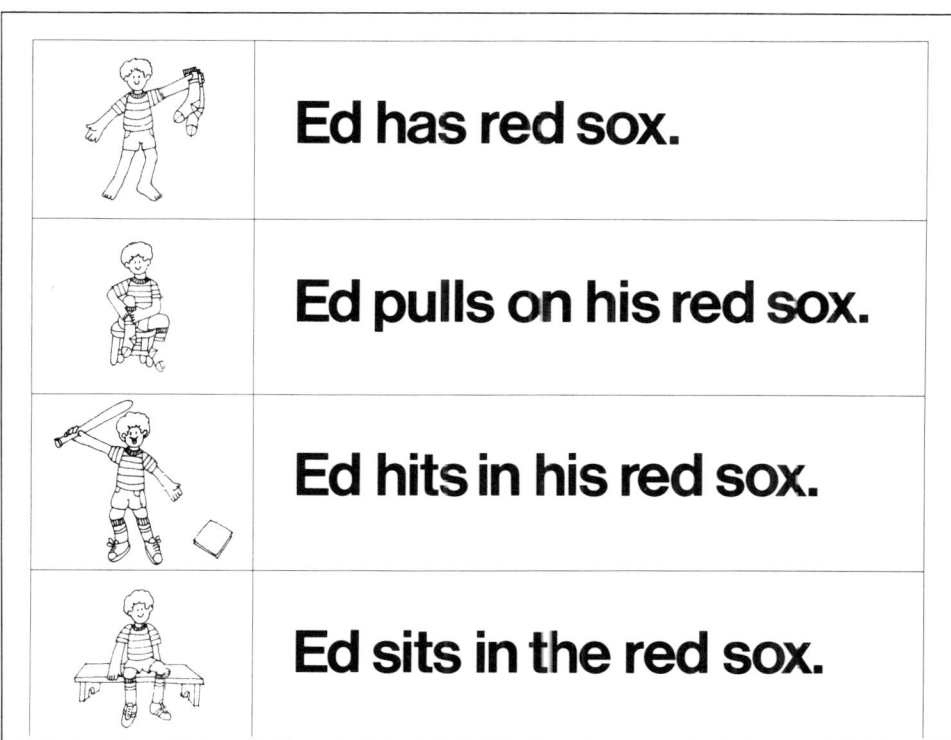

Material for lesson twenty-two: P-71a, b, and c.

Section II.

The Blue Reading Lab Manual

Development in Grammar

Lesson 1:
Longer Nouns

Materials

- the set of longer phonetic word cards from the pink materials packet (sheet number B-50), prepared in the usual way)
- a black box labeled *Nouns, Box 3*
- the heading card on the pack, fastened with a rubber band
- an assigned place on the materials shelf, near *Box 1, Nouns*

Philosophy

This is the beginning of the child's wish to stretch herself, to use to the utmost the power she is creating.

You must now supply her with carefully graded materials to allow her to exercise her growing competence. It is essential that she does this, for it is now that she learns to challenge herself, to explore the lure of ambiguity that will become her greatest spur to self-motivated learning as she develops intellectually.

This section of exercises is designed to challenge the child to use what she has already learned in a harder task, and to insure the success of her efforts by careful programming of the levels of difficulty. Her success will give her a tremendous feeling of self-confidence.

The design of the material may seem inconsequential to the teacher. However, if the material is not understood in the context of the childs' sequential development, you must not neglect teaching it. In terms of the child's growing self-confidence, such neglect would be indefensible.

This section *must* be taught as outlined.

Procedure

Call to you two or three children who are doing well with the *secret words, the verb commands,* and the *sentences and pictures* from the pink reading section.

Using *Nouns, Box 3,* allow the children to choose and to distribute individual noun cards around the room. Each card will be positioned against the object that it names.

Have the children collect the cards and replace them properly in the labeled box. Showing them where it is to be kept, have them put it in its assigned place.

Additional List of Nouns in the Room

This list is presented that the teacher may prepare additional material for the children's use (if the objects are present in the classroom).

These words should be printed with white ink on black card stock of good quality, cut into the regular 2-by-2½-inch size, and added to the black noun box, *Nouns Box 3*.

bulb	handbag	sack
button	lamp	silk
compass	mild	stamp
cotton	nest	steps
felt	pants	umbrella
glass	ribbon	
glasses	rock	

Lesson Two: Exercises for Pencil Control

Materials	▪ designs from the blue reading materials, B-136a, b, c, d, e, and f, reproduced and cut into 5½-by-5½-inch sections, stacked in flat trays or baskets, ready for the child to use at any time ▪ several pencils of varying colors ▪ a child's table
Philosophy	The child's pencil control should now be such that he is able to fill in the two-color designs smoothly, with the parallel lines straight and vertical, lying so closely together that the space is filled with color, no white spaces showing between lines. When this happens, the child is ready for more complicated designs. The object now is to show him the fascination of choosing colors that harmonize to produce a design of beauty. This exercise uses the skill he has been developing in a more advanced way that keeps him interested in the process. His interest encourages growth in pencil-control skill.
Procedure	Take two of the designs to the child's table, one for yourself, one for him. Take as many pencils as you have decided will be needed to produce an interesting color combination. Discuss color with him. Sit with him, giving him a blank pattern, keeping the other for yourself. Begin to color your design, making sure your colors harmonize. Let him work with you on his design. When you have finished, show him where these more advanced designs are kept. Coloring a design will now become part of his daily work. He should be encouraged by your enthusiasm to complete one each day. Do not require it, however, unless the child is over six and has not yet shown good writing control by writing well-shaped, uniform letters.
Timing	If the child has had the initial exercises, he will be able to progress to this level of difficulty by the time he is 4½ years old.

Instructions for Preparing Materials for Lesson Two

Materials	▪ B-77a through f in the blue reading lab materials ▪ one basket or small box for each 5½-inch-by-5½-inch figure ▪ a constant supply of many shades of colored pencils ▪ containers for the pencils
Preparation	Copy onto colored paper sheets B-77a, b, c, d, e, and f of the materials packet. Take these sheets to a copy factory and have them cut into 5½-by-5½-inch sections. Copy factories have the equipment to cut paper with neat precision. The designs may be cut by hand with a sharp paper cutter, but the extra time and work required is hardly worth it. Put a small supply of each design in the boxes, trays, or baskets you have prepared. Store the balance of the designs where they are easily accessible to the children. Keep the supply constant.

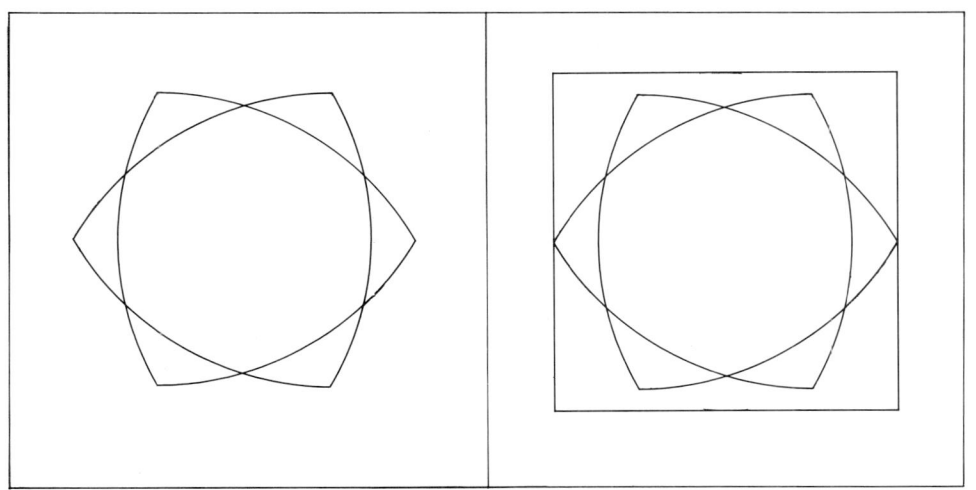
Designs for lesson two: B-77a, b, c, c, e, and f of the blue reading materials.

Lesson Three:
Analysis of Words

Materials
- the coded, movable alphabet
- a 3-by-6-foot rug or mat
- two children who get on well and are doing well with the pink reading material (These children should be reading words and sentences and composing sentences with *Farm One*. They should be showing an interest in writing words, phrases, and sentences of their own.)

Philosophy

Once again the child's natural drive toward solving ambiguities is to be utilized. A child who really knows the first material in the complicated process of learning to read will use her knowledge to conquer the next step, which is to use her now considerable skills to conquer more words.

The only new thing introduced at this time is the *length of the word.* This step is of extreme importance. It must not be neglected or shortened. Only if it is accomplished properly will the child advance with confidence into the most difficult step in learning to read English—the combining of two or more letters to make a new sound.

Therefore, each word in this section is phonetic, each letter standing for only the sound learned with the sandpaper letters.

The child is introduced to these longer words with the process she already knows: constructing the dictated words with the letters of the big movable alphabet.

It is of value to her at this stage in her development to work with another child who has reached a similar stage of development.

You, as teacher, should be quietly enthusiastic.

Procedure

You will invite the two children you select to join you. Have them lay out the mat and place the movable alphabet in position. Sit with the children around the mat.

Using your prepared list, pronounce a word very distinctly: "Jump." Have the children listen to the word, then repeat it. Ask them to look for the sound they heard first and lay it on the mat.

Continue, progressing letter by letter through the word.

Work with two or three more words from the list; then point out to the children that each word has a blue letter in it for the vowel sound. You may tell them the blue letter is a vowel if they are interested, but this is not a necessary part of the child's knowledge at this time. In no way require the child to know that a vowel is a vowel.

Making sure the children are having a good time, continue this level of word-building until the two workers have complete confidence in their ability to hear the sounds in longer words and to select those sounds and assemble the words.

Again let us emphasize that *this is a critical stage in the child's development pattern and must be given careful attention.* The success she has at this stage of her understanding is what fuels her willingness to tackle the much more difficult process of constructing new sounds from letter combinations—a process necessary for her continuing advancement. It is a stage that *must not* be neglected, no matter how repetitious it seems to you.

Timing

Whenever the child shows real confidence with the three-letter, phonetic material coded pink. She should use any of this material with ease and interest and should be handling all grammar material with confidence. Children started at four with the sandpaper letters will normally be reading in about six months.

Word List for Lesson Three:

camp	fond	grunt
fret	cost	wept
step	dent	rent
jump	glad	trap
melt	hand	stamp
silk	drum	stand
trim	bump	slap
grand	must	pink
tank	ribbon	lump
twist	fist	swing
plot	lift	bring
drop	crust	mend
stump	next	west
hunt	wing	land
hang	tint	test
trust	drip	gift
bank	pond	strip
skunk	snap	flax
bulb	rang	desk
drink	sank	flat
lend	spend	frog
tent	went	soft
twig	print	kitten
spot	frost	happen
duck	king	stung

Lesson Four: Objects for Word Building

Materials
- the movable alphabet
- a 3-by-6-foot mat or rug
- a blue-coded box containing six or eight objects that are nouns containing four or more letters (See accompanying list.)

Philosophy The child now has a firm knowledge of the phonetic structure of short three-letter words. At this time he can read, write, and spell on this level of difficulty.

He is now ready to stretch toward the next level. He needs to learn he is capable of doing this level on his own. In order for him to realize this fully, take him back into familiar processes. In this way, he can gain confidence in his ability to attack a new concept and solve it on his own. He validates his own learning, furthering his ability to guide his intrinsic drive toward overcoming difficulties as they present themselves. The confidence he gains now leads him to explore his own potential in a manner that is amazing.

Procedure Place the mat on the floor and arrange the materials in the usual order.

Talk with the child about the objects in the box. Let him arrange them down the side of his mat as he has been taught.

Let him sound the word and form it. Point out the necessity of having one vowel in each word. Do not overteach.

Let him share with you what he does if he wishes.

Do not demand accuracy, but be aware if the child repeatedly makes errors. If he does not correct himself in time, have some more sessions in which you call out words, and he listens and forms them with the letters (lesson three).

Timing The child will need to have been working very well with the three-letter techniques before he is introduced to this work. He also should have had a number of sessions of spelling as the teacher calls out words. He must be able to do lesson three successfully before he is given this lesson.

Instructions for Preparing Materials for Lesson Four

Materials
- several small boxes, coded blue, at least 3-by-3-by-2½ inches, labeled *Blue, Set 1*
- six or eight small objects in each box (taken from the list below)

List of objects (These may be plastic, wooden or metal, but the colors should be true colors and the objects not misshapen but true miniatures.)

bull
stamp
bolt
ring
clamp
clip (paper clip)
drum
basket

This list is suggested only and should not be used as a restricted list. Any object of four or more letters, in which each letter naming it stands for only one sound, will do. Use no objects whose letters combine to make a different sound, such as bear, pail, cow, and others.

Progression in Writing and Word Building

Lesson Five: Illustrating and Writing

Materials
- a large tray
- a supply of 12-by-18-inch blank newsprint
- a pencil
- crayons or other media the child may choose for her illustrating

Philosophy

The child who is this far along in her learning will enjoy illustrating an incident or something of importance to her. This exercise is used to begin her awareness that she is able to think of something, write it down, and share it with others.

She will use words that are not phonetic. Write these for her until such time as she becomes able to use the dictionary.

Procedures

Give the child a piece of blank paper. Ask her to draw a picture about anything she would like to have you see. Make absolutely no comment on these pictures. Accept whatever she tells you about her effort.

When she has finished with her picture, sit with her and ask her if she can tell you a story about her picture.

Write her name clearly, preferably in the upper right-hand corner of the paper. Ask her if she would like to have you write her story for her. At first, these stories will probably be short one-liners. You must insure that they are complete sentences, written properly, with spacing between words and with capitalization and good punctuation. *But the story must be the child's own.*

Call attention to spacing between words, elaborating by placing your finger between the words to make adequate spacing.

Read the story back to the child. Ask her to read it to you, guiding her hand along the sentence in an even manner.

If another child listens, ask the author if the on-looker may read her story.

Tell the child you are going to make a book for her. Each time she writes a story, add it to her book. Have her read each story each day.

Extension

In a week or ten days, send the pictures home and start a new book.

When the child asks for her story to be written, say to her: "You know, I am sure you can write your story yourself." From this point onward, have her write all the phonetic words she voices in her story. She will soon reach the point at which she will come to you only for the words that puzzle her. If she has the tools to write these words, point it out to her.

If the word embodies combinations of letters with sounds she does not know, write the word on a little slip of paper and let her transfer it to her sentence.

Note

The next step will be for the child to learn to use her first dictionary. But unless she demands it, she is not yet ready to begin.

Lesson Six: Pictured Objects and the Coded Alphabet

Materials
- several prepared boxes of pictured objects, only one for each lesson
- the coded alphabet
- a floor mat or a rug

Preparation Copy sheet with B-83a, b, and c from the blue materials section.
Contact both front and backs of copies.
Cut contacted cards into regular size.
Assemble cards into six or eight boxes coded blue, between six and eight cards in each box. Use a random selection of vowels.

Note As we warned previously, do not give the child sets of words separated according to the vowel sound. It slows his natural progress.

Philosophy The child is acquainted with the technique of advancement through this stage of his understanding. He is not familiar with the necessity of holding sounds in his mind through longer phonetic words. This material gives a firm background for experiencing growing power to conquer unknown words.

If he is to be freed for real reading, he must be willing to tackle unknown words, no matter what their length.

Because you will keep the longer words absolutely phonetic at this time, the child has only the one difficulty to overcome: the length of the word. This stage must be given him so that his confidence in his ability has no setback.

Procedure Invite the child to work with you.
Arrange the materials in the usual manner.
Because the child is acquainted with the technique, stay with him only long enough to insure that he feels confident.

Again, remember that this is the child's first work and is a mechanical, oral spelling that has not yet become reading. He must not be required to read his work to you, although he will often do this. When he wishes to do so, let him, but his reading, on this level, must be entirely voluntary.

Timing After the child can use the alphabet and the objects that are longer phonetic words to compose his own words.

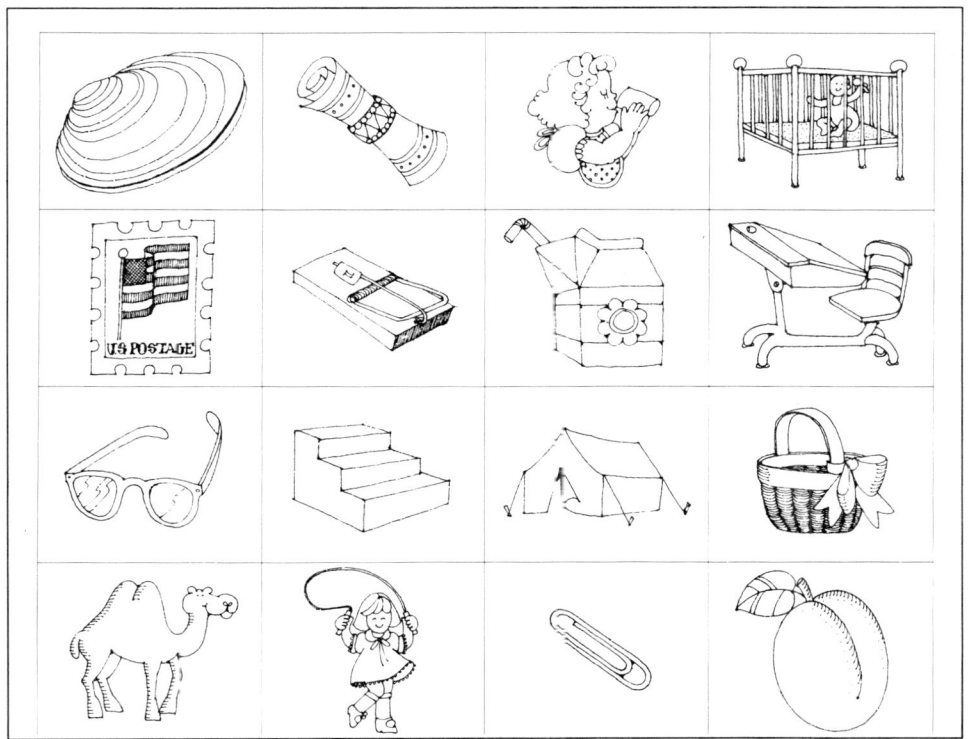

Materials for lesson six: B-83a, b, and c of the blue reading materials.

Lesson Seven: Objects and Word Cards

Materials
- several boxes coded blue, each box to contain six or eight objects taken from the following list of longer phonetic nouns
- a child's table
- a small mat

Philosophy The child has learned to manipulate and assemble large movable letters into words. We now give her the words and lead her into the more abstract act of relating the word to the concrete object.

Procedure Take one box of objects to the child's table. The word cards for the objects will be in the box.

Place a mat on the floor of a size to hold her work and sit with her while she arranges the objects below each other, down the left-hand edge of the mat.

Hand her the first card. Listen as she sounds the word and puts the sounds together.

Let her place the card beside the appropriate object.

Leave her as soon as she is sure of the technique.

Timing The child is ready when she can arrange the letters and pictures.

Additional List of Nouns for Object and Word Boxes:

This list is prepared to assist you in collecting additional objects so that the child will have an adequate, varied supply when she begins this phase of her work.

All objects are to be distributed in blue coded boxes, at random. A packet of blue word cards must be prepared from card stock, one card for each object in the box. These cards will be cut to the standard 2-by-2½-inch size.

Each blue box containing this material should be labeled *Objects and Words*, with the number recorded on the lid.

belt	lamp
bonnet	mitten
bulb	nuts
clock	plum
club	pump
crab	ring
gift	skunk
glass	tongs
gull	trumpet

This is a suggested list only. You may be able to find other objects.

Please be cautioned that only phonetic objects may be used at this level of understanding. Each letter *must* stand for the one sound the child learned during the lesson on sandpaper letters.

Lesson Eight:
Large Picture Cards
and Word Cards

■ one of the large eight-by-ten-inch cards containing eight pictures ■ a set of small word cards containing printed words for the pictures ■ a child's work table	Materials
The child needs now to progress toward the more abstract, working with the difficult longer phonetic words. In this set of materials, only the words are loose, needing to be placed under the stationary picture of an object that has a completely phonetic name—the only obstacle that of length.	Philosophy
Take the material to the child's table and have him lay it out as he has been shown. Select any card and hand it to the child. Ask him to read it and find the picture it names. Make sure he feels confident, then leave him to his task.	Procedure
Any time after the child can be successful with the pictures and the alphabet.	Timing

Instructions for Preparing Materials for Lesson Eight

■ word cards B-86a, d, g, j, and m in the blue reading materials packet ■ large cards B-86b, c, e, f, h, i, k, l, n, and o in the blue packet ■ contact paper ■ rubber bands ■ small envelopes ■ paper clips	Materials
Prepare the cards as you have done previously. Assign the material to its permanent place on the reading shelves.	Preparation

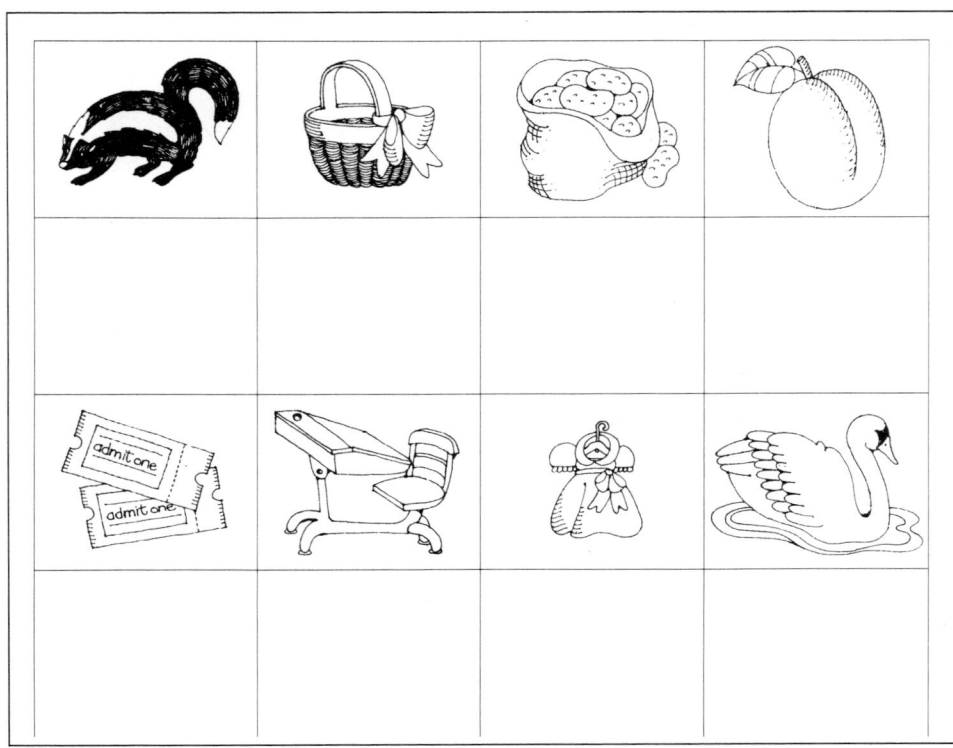

These picture cards are used with lesson eight: B-86b, c, e, f, h, i, k, l, n, and o. The word cards are B-86a, d, g, j, and m.

Lesson Nine:
Loose Picture Cards
and Word Cards

Materials
- one of the blue boxes of loose pictures and word cards prepared for this level of difficulty
- a child's work table

Philosophy

The child now strengthens her growing ability to freely associate the picture as a symbol, the word as a further abstraction of that symbol. She is at this time reaching out, getting farther away from the technique of mechanical spelling as opposed to the skills of real reading.

You will find that some children make the leap into real reading very soon now, although most will still not make the extra growth for some time yet. The special needs of both types of children must be carefully noted and cared for.

Procedure

Take a box to the child's table. She knows how to lay the picture in a horizontal row across the top of her table. Allow her to do this, talking about any picture she may not know.

Hand the pack of word cards to her and let her deal with them.

If she needs assistance, give it to her.

Leave her as soon as possible, making sure she knows where to place the materials on the shelf.

Timing

When the child shows competence with materials preceding this.

Instructions for Preparing the Materials for Lesson Nine

Materials
- the word and picture cards: B-88a, b, c, and d in the blue reading materials packet
- contact paper
- rubber bands
- set of boxes, coded blue

Preparation

Prepare the pictures and contact them. Cut each sheet into 2-by-2½-inch cards.

Divide them into sets, eight pictures and eight of the corresponding word cards in each set.

Fasten them with rubber bands and place each set in its own box.

Assign the material to its proper place on the reading shelf.

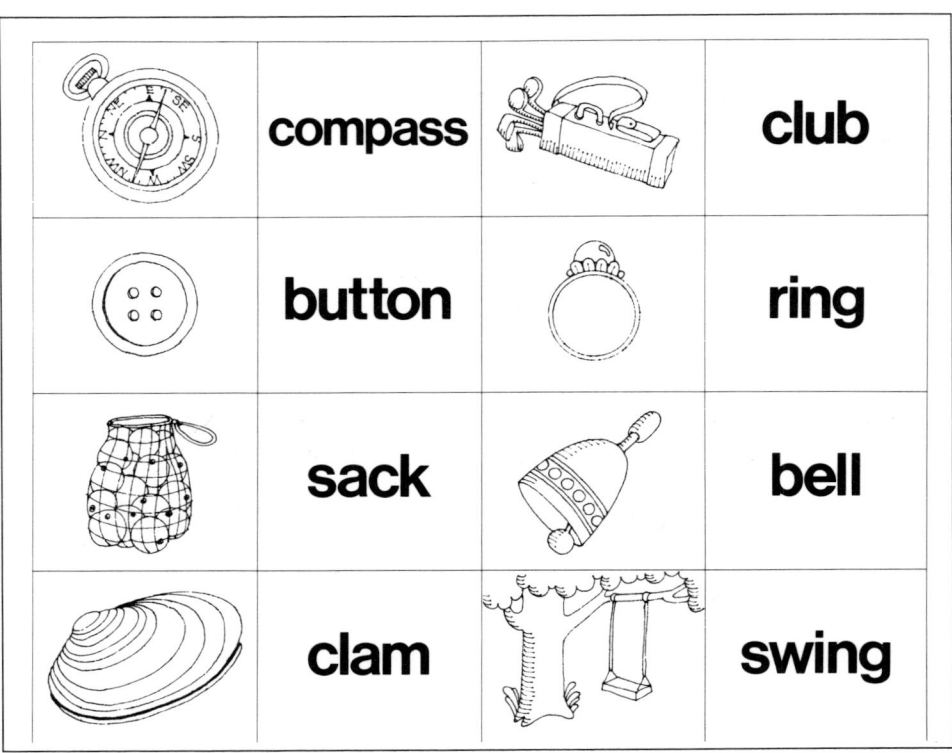

These cards are used with lesson nine: B-88a, b, c, and d.

Lesson Ten: Longer Nouns, Farm One

Piquing the Child's Interest

When several children are working as individuals with the farm materials, add more objects with longer phonetic names to the box. If possible, all the objects added should be related to the rest of the objects. The following list is presented to aid in their selection.

wagon	well	duckling	kitten
rabbit	windmill	piglet	bucket
grass	cock	bull	pond
pump	duck	milk	frog

These nouns should be kept in a separate stack with a separate heading card. From time to time, add verbs and adjectives to the farm box.

Do not add the nouns, verbs, and adjectives all at once. The additional words are in the materials packet. The child has much greater enjoyment if the additions come in small increments.

Lesson Eleven:
Verb Commands

For Further Understanding

Through the use of the grammar materials in this integrated language arts approach, the child is given an understanding of the use of grammar from the outset. This understanding is such that it is unnecessary to program her through cumbersome and often less than effective conventional ways of teaching comprehension and creative interpretation.

By this stage of her development, she should have had enough experience with the "puzzle" words that she recognizes them as sight words. These forty-six words do not conform to the structure of the program to this point, yet are words that she uses constantly and needs to know.

You, as teacher, will use them at this time in the next step in the child's advancement toward reading independence. You now construct sentence commands on slips of paper to be given to the child. She reads the command and performs the action without any exchange of words.

She should at this time have begun to integrate the meaning of the written word. If she has been having daily experience with the verb commands, either on an individual basis or with a friend or two, she should be able to interpret these more complicated commands. To this point, you should not have involved yourself in the child's interpretation of verb commands, leaving critical comment and further exploration of individual verb meaning to come from the child's peers as they work together.

You now need to assess the effectiveness of the child's learning. Do this by writing more complicated verb commands on slips of paper. Give these to the child one at a time. She reads her slip without help and performs the actions called for.

You must observe her to see if she shows confidence and if she is making good progress in her free interpretation of the written instruction. If you find the child is not yet ready for the more complicated instructions, have two or three simple instructions prepared so that you are able to back away without upsetting the child or making her anxious.

You must insure that the child who was not ready works with the *Verb Commands, Box 1 and 2,* each day. You might have to work with these early boxes as group games several times to renew the unsuccessful child's interest.

Some Suggestions for Verb Command Slips

You must add to these suggestions, which should be written on white slips of paper and cut to uniform size. They should be stored in a box or a basket, coded red, and labeled.

Run to the desk and skip back.
Jog to the clock. Put a hand on it.
Skip to a girl. Pat the girl's hand.
Get the bell and ring it.
Bring the oldest boy in this class to my desk.
Bend your leg and kick it up.
Sit on the rug and hum a song.
Get a pen and jot ten dots on a long pink or red slip.
Laugh at a friend.
Put a plant on my desk.

Slip a clip on a pad.
Tap your leg with a pen.
Sniff at a plant.
Sip a drink from a cup. Put the cup up.
Sit on the rug and rock.
Hum a song to a friend.
Slip a pen in your pocket and skip to a friend.
Select a flag. Hop to a friend. Put it in his hand.
Hug a boy. Hop and skip with him.

Lesson Twelve: Blue Word Lists

Materials — one of the blue word lists

Philosophy — The child now tries his ability at identifying longer phonetic words without the aid of pictures or objects. This is an important step in his development; it serves to confirm his ability to master words with unknown sound combinations. It is not a step to be ignored if the child is to gain confidence in his ability to apply his skills to new materials.

Procedure — Take one of the word lists to the child's table and ask him to read it. Let him know many more lists are available, and allow him to set his own pace.

Timing — When he is handling the loose pictures and words well.

Instructions for Preparing Materials for Lesson Twelve

Materials
- long blue cards: B-93a, b, c, d, and e of the blue materials packet
- a paper punch
- ten lengths of eighteen-inch blue wool yarn
- contact paper
- scissors

Preparation
- Copy the blue reading list from the packet of blue materials.
- Contact uncut sheets on both sides.
- Punch two holes on the top edge of each list, thread them with a length of blue yarn, and tie them. Do this for each list.
- Hang the cards on hooks in the classroom language area, two or three to a hook.

hump	bent
insist	land
timid	windmill
expect	picnic
swag	stop
velvet	glum
bled	madcap
hubbub	strand
punt	grin
blond	helmet

These lists are to be used with lesson twelve of the blue reading lab B-93a, b, c, d, and e.

Lesson Thirteen: Secret Words

Materials	one of the prepared blue secret boxes
Philosophy	This material serves to confirm the child's confidence in her own ability to apply that which she knows to unknown combinations of sounds. It is necessary that she be provided with this positive reinforcement as she approaches the problems presented by the nonphonetic portions of English words. Again, it is of utmost importance that the child be given this positive concept of self and of her own ability to conquer the unknown if she is to maintain her easy advance through the materials that follow these.
Procedure	The child will know the techniques of handling the secret boxes. Take the first box to her, get her started, and point out the supply available. She should be able to go on without further help.
Timing	As soon as the child is able and confident in her approach to words that have no picture clue.

Instructions for Preparing Materials for Lesson Thirteen

Materials	■ the set of blue word lists: B-95a, b, c, d, e, f, g, h, i, and j ■ a ruler and a pencil ■ five boxes: suggested size 3½-by-3½-by-2 inches ■ scissors or a paper cutter ■ light blue spray enamel
Preparation	Spray the boxes blue and set them aside to dry. With a ruler, divide the sheets into four equal squares. Fold the resulting slips into small squares and place eight of the folded squares into each of the boxes. Label each box top *Secret Box.* Assign the boxes to their places on the reading shelf.

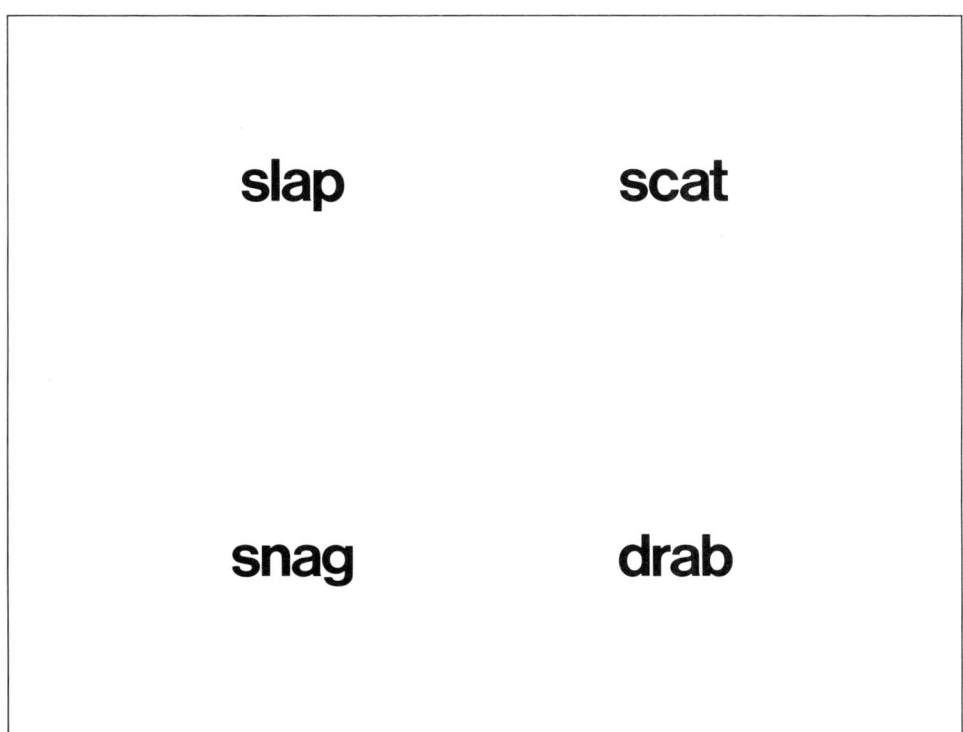

Word slips for Secret Box

Appendix A: Continued Reading Development

To Implement the Child's Progress

To the teacher of the preschool child who has used this program and finds that his charges are wanting to read *books,* we wish to present some ideas for furthering their development.

I

Let each child construct books consisting of her own illustrations and the stories she has written to go with them.

As we have suggested, in the beginning the child dictates these stories to the teacher, who writes them on the illustration.

This is part of the construction of the cohesive thought process. The child is *never* forced to copy or read these stories, although she often expresses a strong desire to read. The teacher always reads the whole story the child has dictated to him.

As the child progresses, the teacher begins to give her the responsibility of constructing her own story, pointing out to her that she can write any of the phonetic words she needs. The teacher supplies the nonphonetic words, written on a slip of paper from which the child can copy.

At this level of growth, never correct a child's written word, no matter what the spelling. The important aspect of her growing development is the thought process. She must not be worried by details at this point.

As she writes her own words, the important detail for the teacher to work on is that she group her letters into the words she wants. Spacing is important now, and the teacher must see that the child does learn how to do it.

Do not mark up the child's paper with corrections!

II

Begin to pay attention to the detail in the child's picture. Important now are open-ended, nonthreatening conversations with him. These conversations should help the child focus on what he is doing, but you should make no attempt to direct him. The fact, gently pointed out over a period of time, that most houses sit upon the ground and not in the air will ultimately have the child looking critically at his production. His buildings will cease being airborne.

III

In order to keep the child's interest aroused in the materials, you, as teacher, must keep adding to the existing items on the reading shelves. In the beginning, do not put out all of the materials constructed from the reading packets.

Add appropriate pieces of materials as you come across them.

Keep in daily touch with the child's use of the materials. Show interest in what she plans to do that day. If her interest seems to lag and is in need of stimulation, give her limited choices in casual conversation, such as the following: "Well, Susan. When you are reading today, are you going to do word lists or large picture cards?"

In creative writing, your question can be something like this: "I really liked the story you wrote yesterday. Was it a continued story? What is the monster going to do today?"

IV

Many children will express a desire to read a book, and you will have to have a good variety of single copies of preprimers available. Never have more than one or two copies of a title in the room. Having to await a turn to read a book adds to the spice of learning to read.

The teacher must *never* limit preprimer reading to strictly phonic readers. This deadly kind of monotony stunts a child's interest in solving word difficulties and can, in time, convince the child any reading that is not phonic is much too difficult.

In the proper preprimer reading the child will encounter words he cannot read. This problem is easily solved. The teacher reads with the child every day, at his request. This reading is always on an individualized basis. The teacher writes on a slip of paper any nonphonetic word in the story the child is reading. He uses all the words he needs to know to read the story. Before he begins the story, the teacher teaches these words with the three-period lesson. These words are given to the child, and he reviews them each day until he knows them. They are then discarded, being replaced by new words each day. If he does not recognize a new word when he comes upon it in a story, the teacher supplies it.

The teacher keeps a card on the child's reading, recording the book he is reading and the pages he reads.

After a child finishes a book, he should be allowed to read it to someone—a parent or another child.

V

The child is now ready to attack the more difficult letter combinations of the English language. These techniques are specialized, and no attempt has been made to include them in this preschool volume.

Neither does the scope of this volume lend itself to the delineation of those techniques necessary for the child's continuing development in grammar, composition, and handwriting. Formal spelling needs to be introduced soon, but it is not included here.

That is not to say that the techniques in this volume cannot be used with older children. Teachers will find this manual of great value in helping any older nonreader. The materials are also of inestimable aid in teaching a child from a bilingual home.

Appendix B:
A compilation of words used in this text

Please note:
1. Bracketed words are puzzle words that do not fit into the phonetic pattern of the English language.
2. Some of these are words that a child learns to recognize by being taught directly through the three-period lesson because he does not possess the tools to decipher them at this time.

A
[a]
add
[adjective]
am
[an]
[April]
[are]
[article]
as
at
[August]
ax

B
bad
bag
band
bang
basin
basket
bat
beg
bell
belt
Ben
bend
bent
best
bet
bib
big
bit
bland
bled
bog
bonnet
box
brag
brat
brig
brim
brittle
bucket

bug
built
bulb
bull
bump
bun
bus
bust
but
buzz

C
camel
camp
can
cannot
cat
clam
clamp
clap
clock
clog
clot
club
cock
cod
comet
compass
cotton
crab
cram
crept
crib
crop
cross
cub
cup
cutup

D
dad
dam
Dan
[December]

desk
did
dim
din
dog
doll
Donna
dot
drab
drag
drink
drinking
drum
duck
dump
dung

E
Ed
egg
eldest
elf
elk
elm
[enough]
expand
expect

F
fan
fast
[February]
fed
felt
fill
fin
fist
fit
fix
flag
fled
fling
fran
fred

fret
[Friday]
[friend]
frock
frog
from

G
gag
gap
gas
get
gift
gig
[girl]
glad
glasses
glum
gob
got
grab
grass
grim
grin
grip
gruff
grunts
grunting
gulp
gum
gun
gust
gutless

H
had
ham
hand
handbag
happen
hat
held
helmet
hen

99

hid
him
hint
hiss
hisses
hissing
hit
hog
hop
hot
hotspot
hubub
huff
hug
hum
humdrum
hump
hut

I
[I]
imp
in
infant
inhibit
inset
insipid
[is]

J
Jack
[January]
jet
jig
job
jog
jot
[July]
jump
[June]
just

K
keg
kept
kick
kid
king
kiss
kit

L
lad
lamp
land
lap
[laugh]
led
lemon
lend

lept
let
lid
limp
lip
lisp
little
lock
long
longer
lost
lot
lump

M
mad
madcap
map
man
[March]
mask
mat
[May]
melt
men
mend
mess
met
milk
mix
mom
[Monday]
mop
[my]

N
nag
Nan
nap
napkin
neglect
net
nib
not
[noun]
[November]
nun
nut

O
off
[October]
on
[one]
ox

P
pad
pat
peg

pen
pet
pick
picnic
pig
piglet
pink
pins
pip
pit
pod
pop
pot
plant
plod
plum
plug
[plural]
prim
prop
puff
puffed
pulling
pulls
pump
pumpkin
pun
pup
putrid

R
rabbit
rack
rag
ram
ran
rank
rap
rat
rested
ribbon
rim
ring
risk
rob
rock
rod
romp
rotten
rub
rug
rum
run
running
runt
rut

S
sack
sag

Sam
sampan
sandman
sap
sat
[Saturday]
scan
scat
Scot
scrip
send
self
[September]
set
silk
sing
[singular]
sink
sip
sit
sits
six
skin
skull
skunk
slack
slap
slept
slim
slip
slit
slot
smell
snack
snag
snap
snub
snug
sock
sod
soft
song
sop
sox
spin
spirit
spit
spot
spotted
spud
stag
stamp
stand
stiff
stinking
stop
strand
strap
stun
[Sunday]

T
tack
tag
tap
tapping
tank
tax
tell
ten
tent
ticket
timid
tin
tint
tip
[that]
[the]
[their]
[there]
[they]
[this]
[Thursday]
[to]
Tom
ton
top
trap
trod
trot
tub
tug
tusk
twig
twin
twist
[two]

U
umbrella
up
us

V
van
vat
velvet
vest
vex
vexed
[verb]
vet
vim
vivid

W
wag
wagon
[was]
web
[Wednesday]
wed
well
went
wept
wet
[were]
[what]
[where]
[who]
wig
will
win
wind
windmill
wink
wit

Y
yap
yell
yelp
yes
yet
[you]

Section III.

Packet for Colored Materials

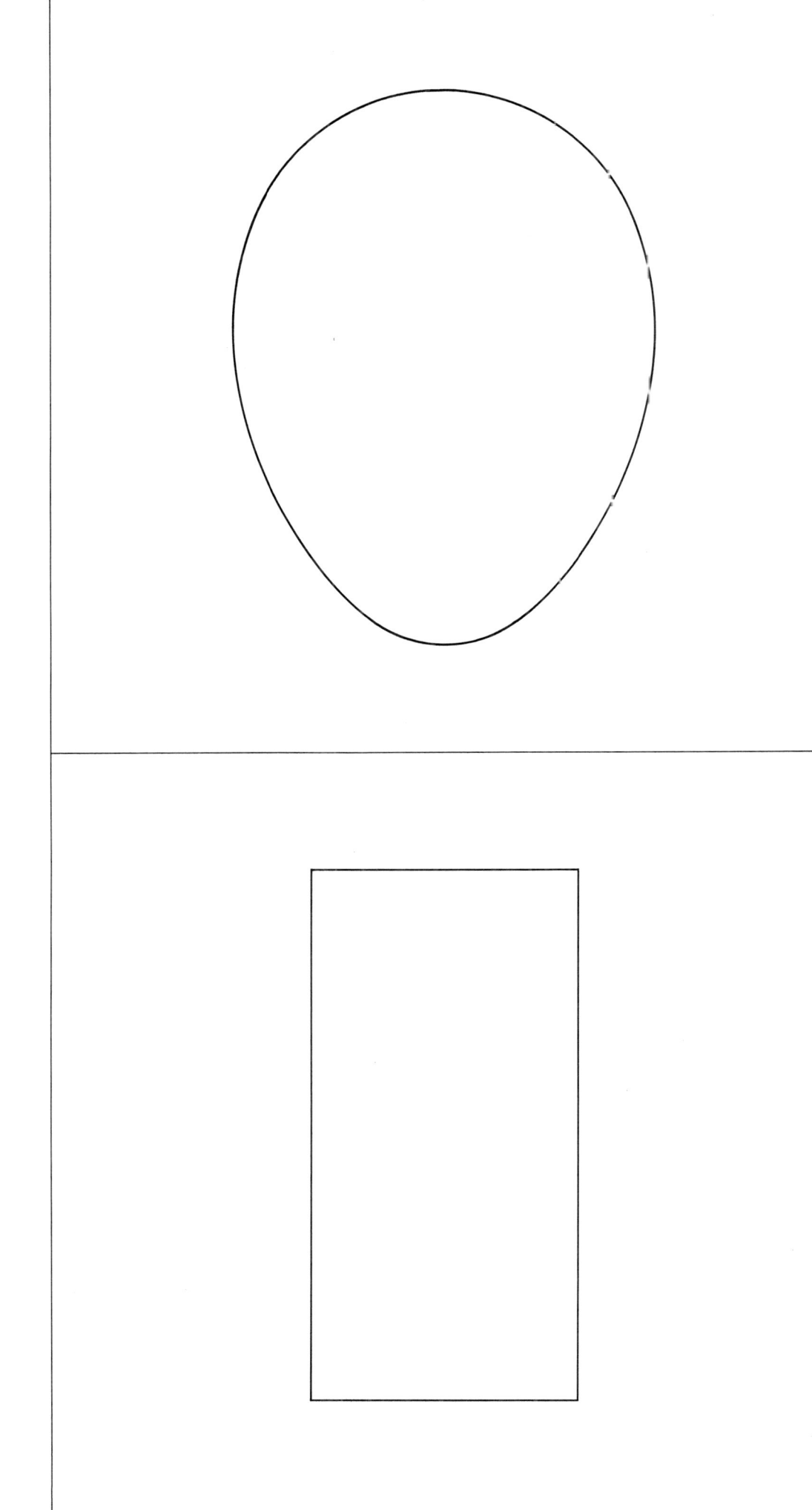

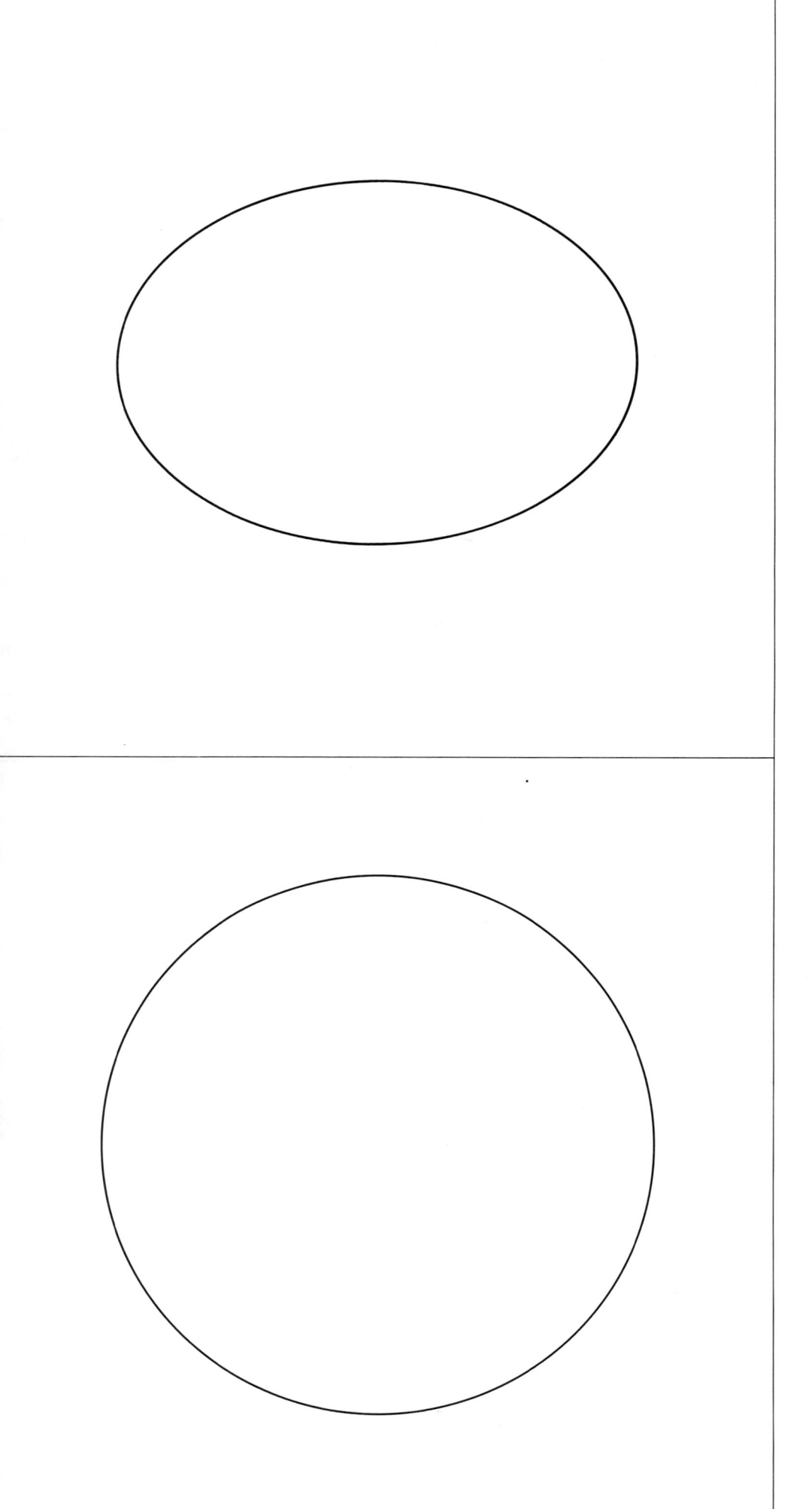

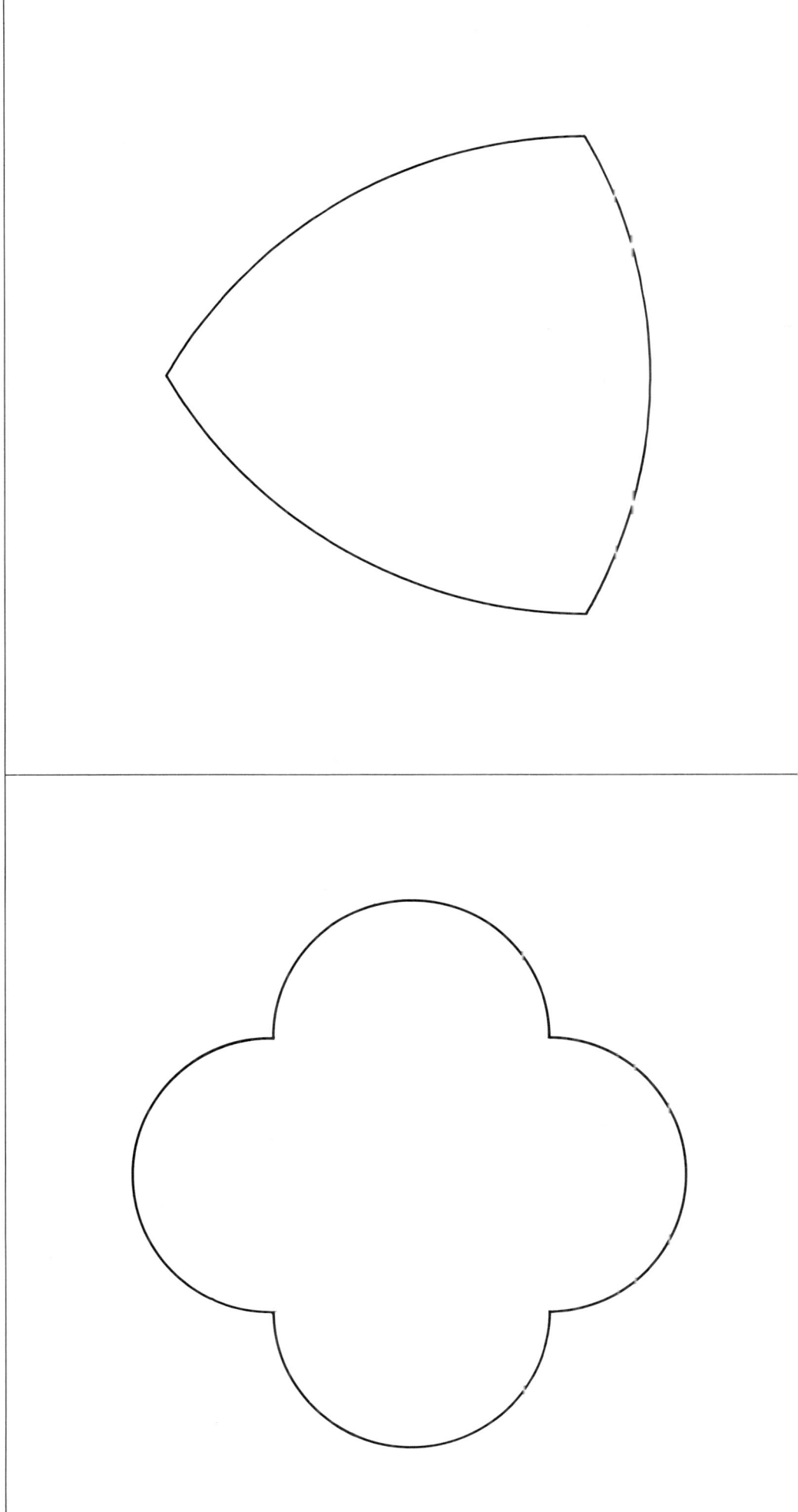

P-24-a Copy this sheet on white paper.

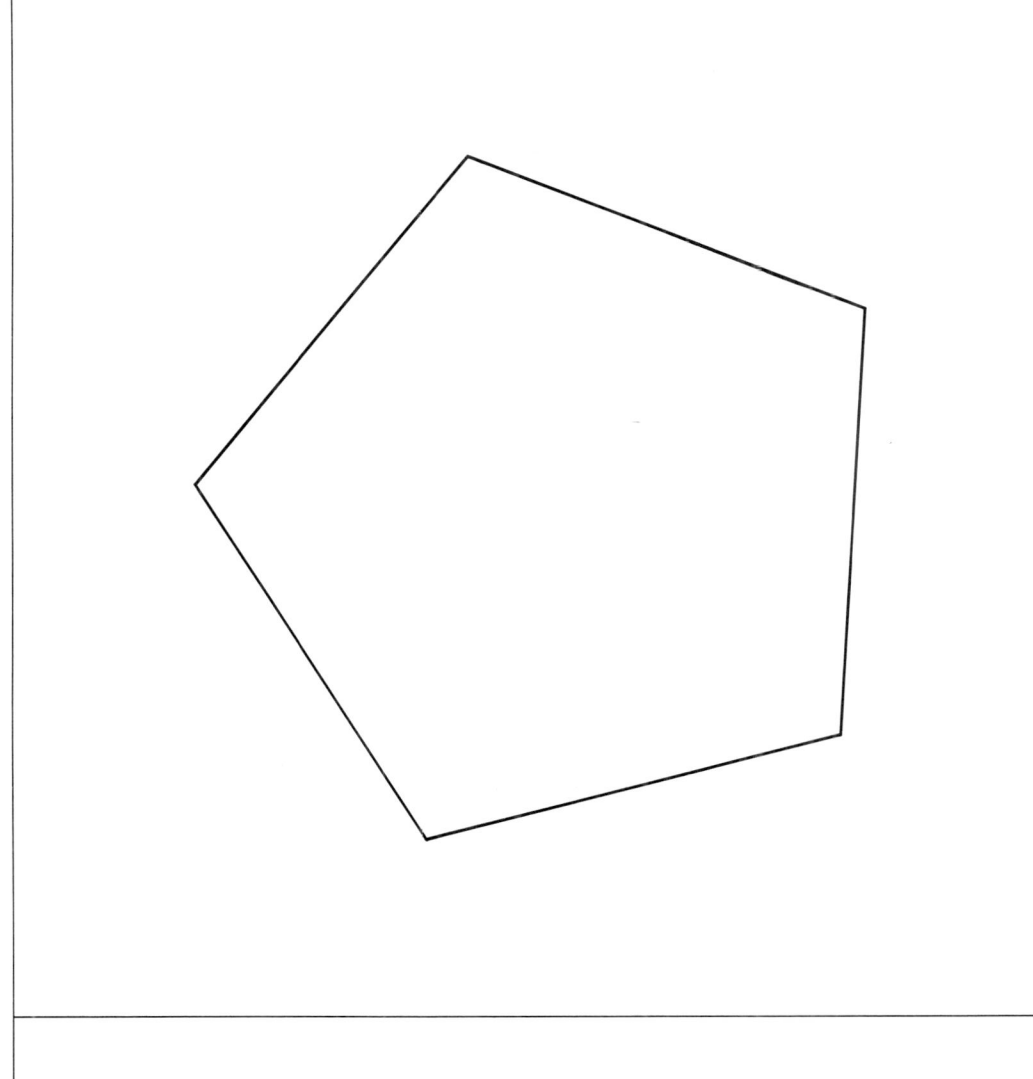
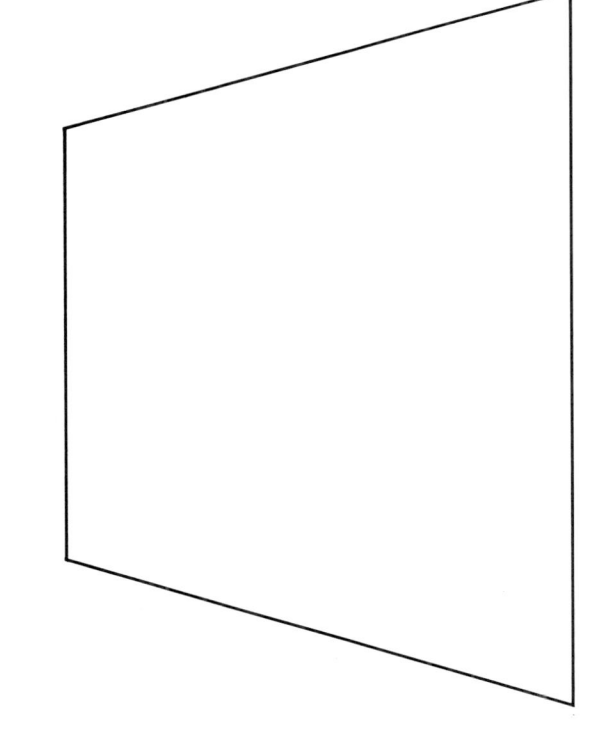

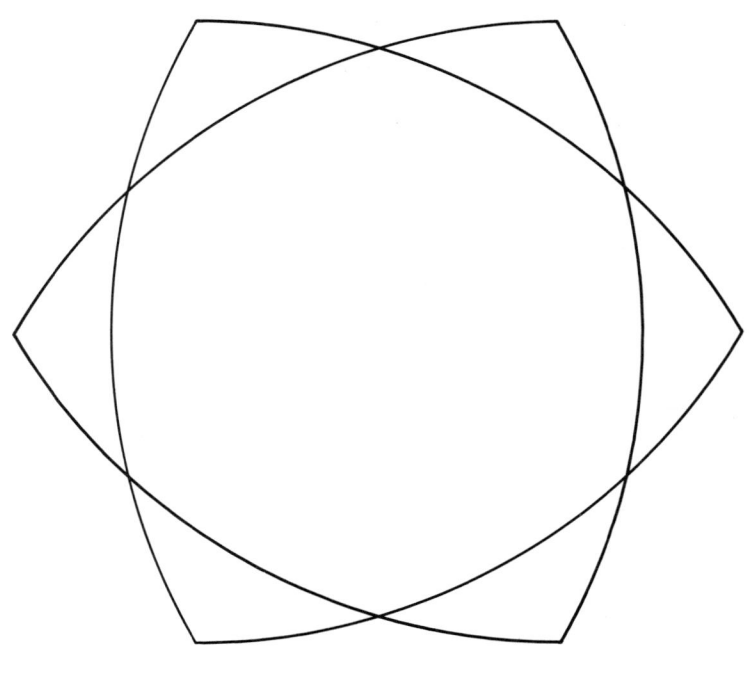
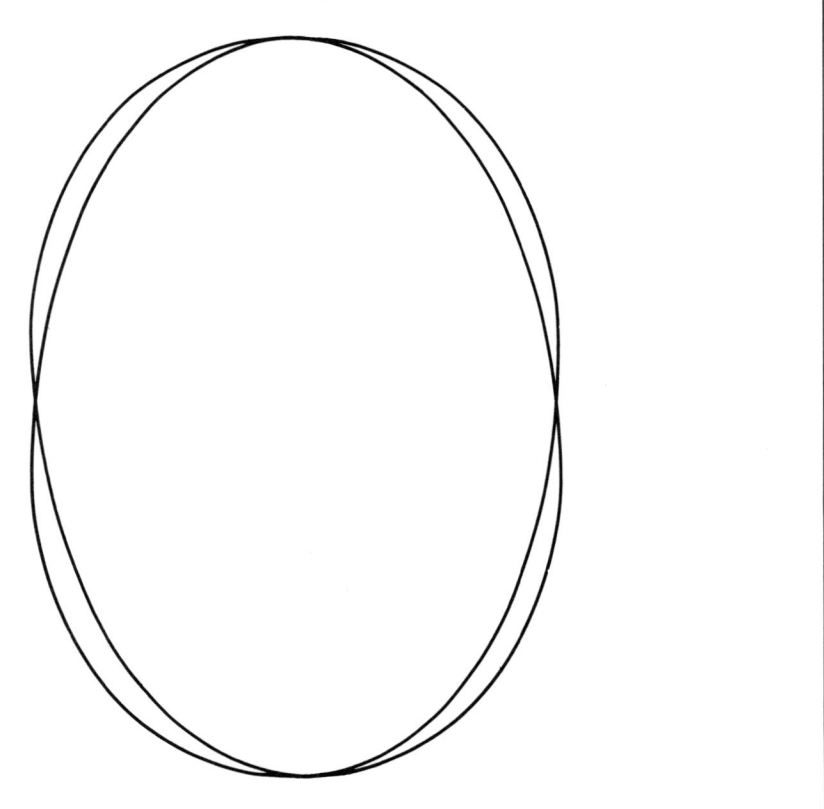

P-24-f Copy this sheet on white paper.

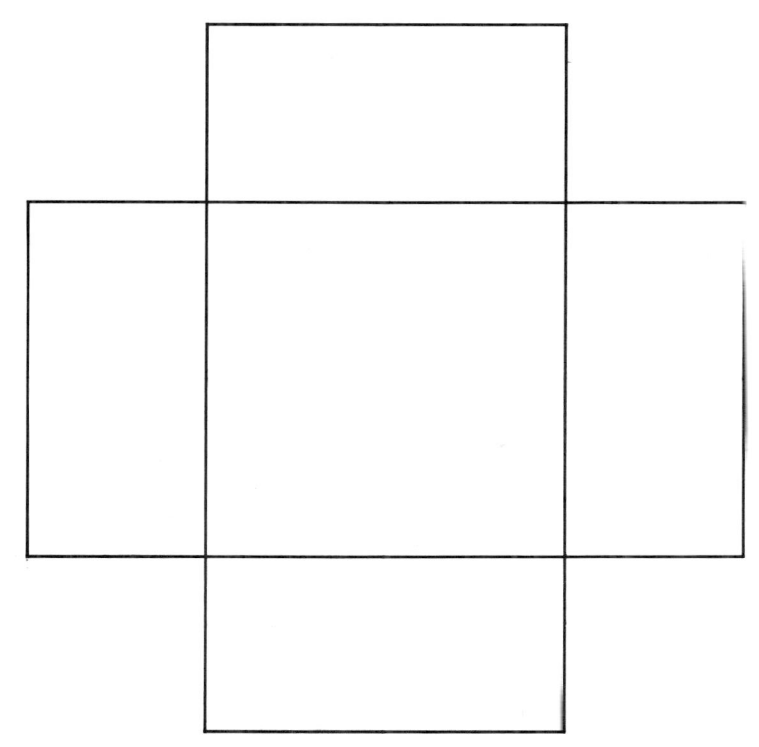

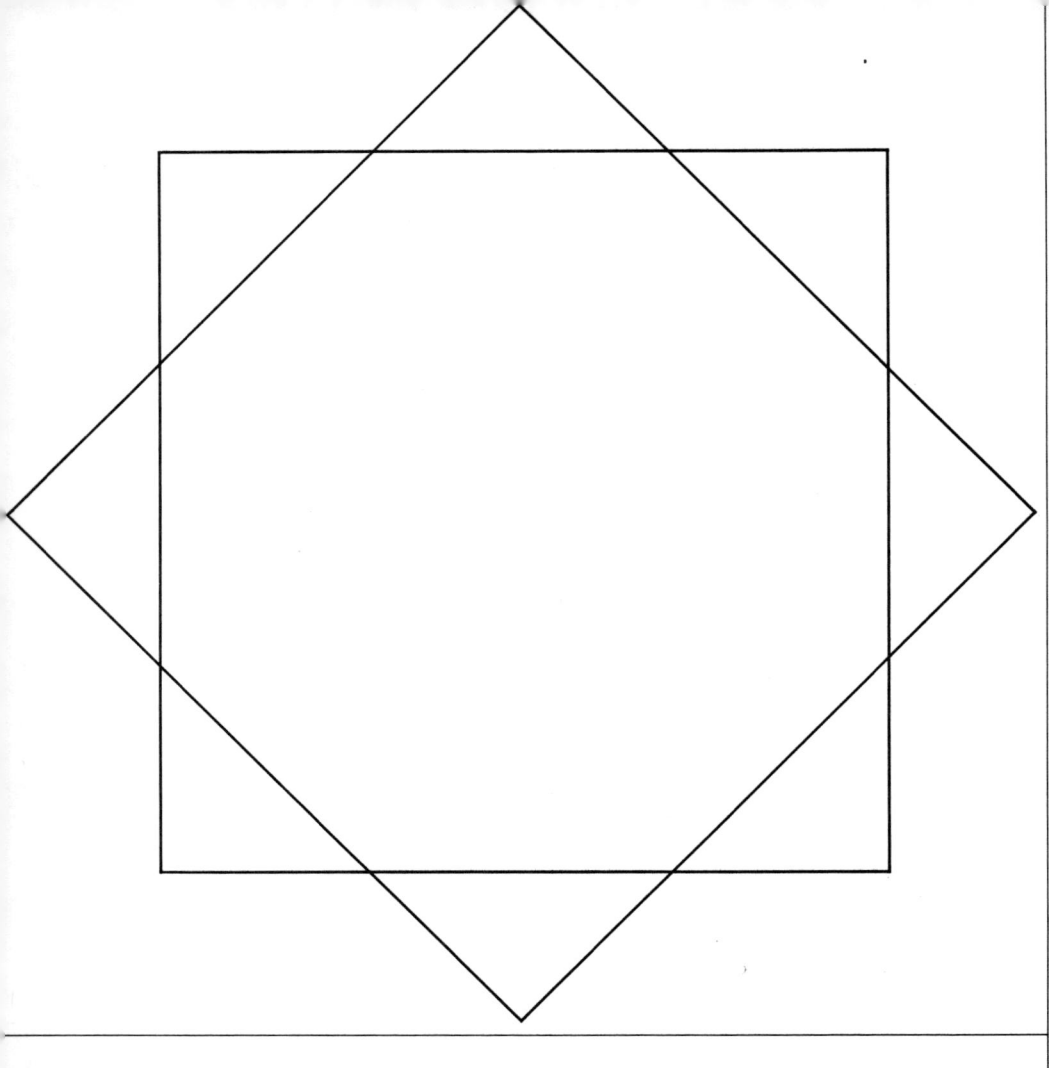

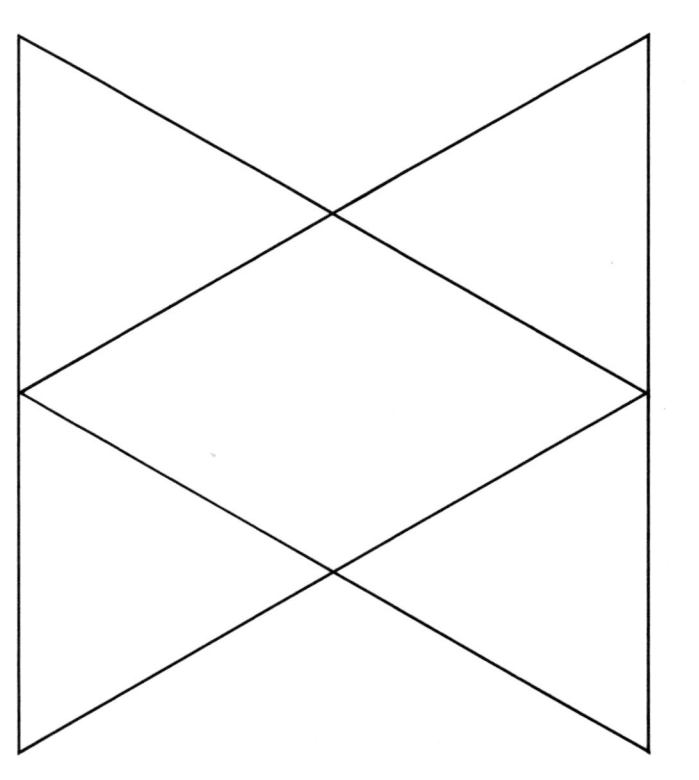

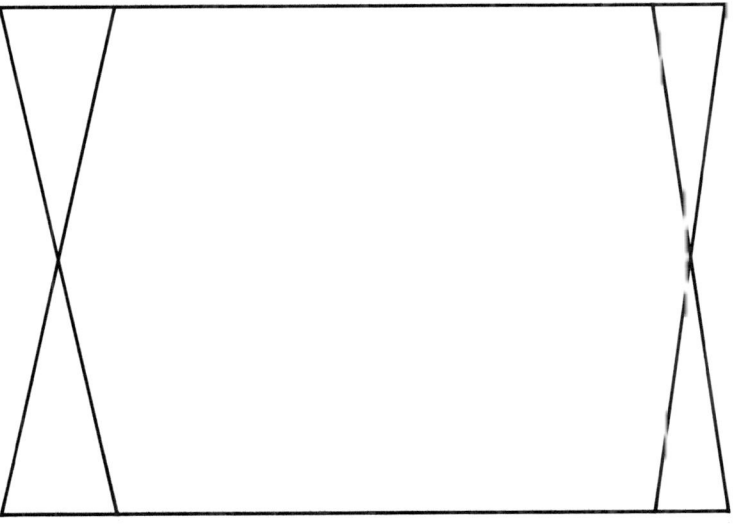

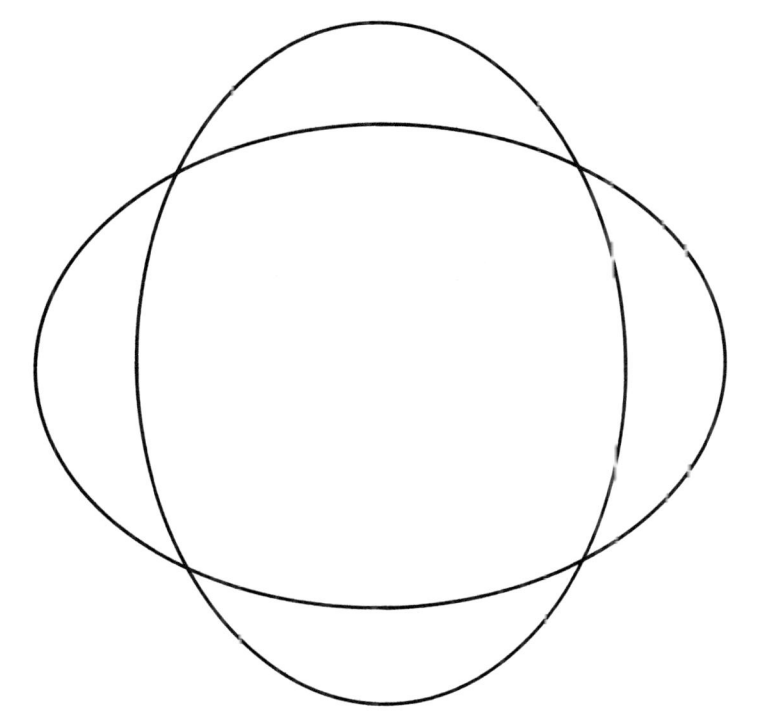

A B C D E F G H I J K
L M N O P Q R S T U V W
X Y Z
a b c d e f g h i j
k l m n o p q r s t u v
w x y z

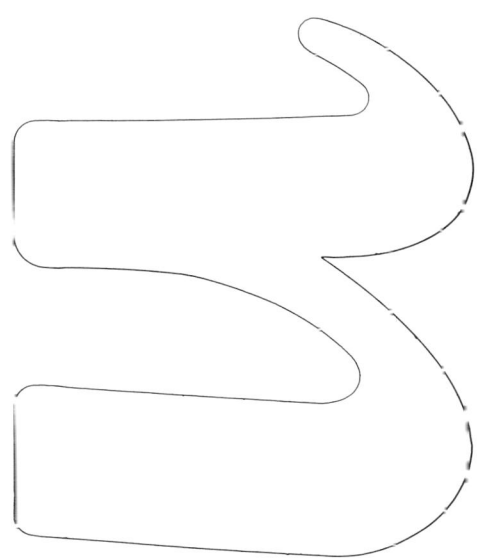

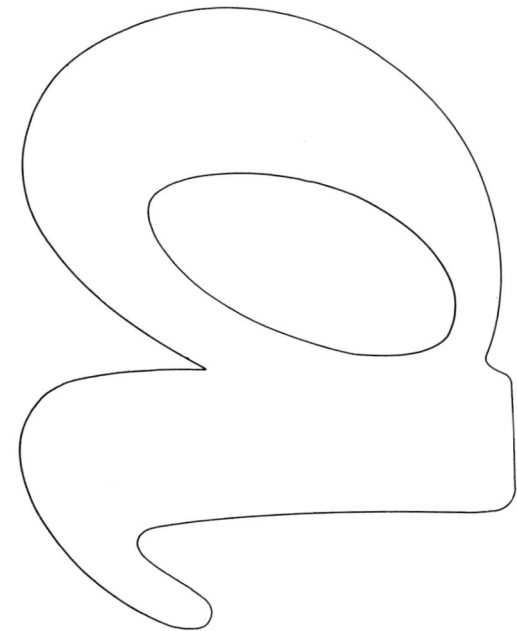
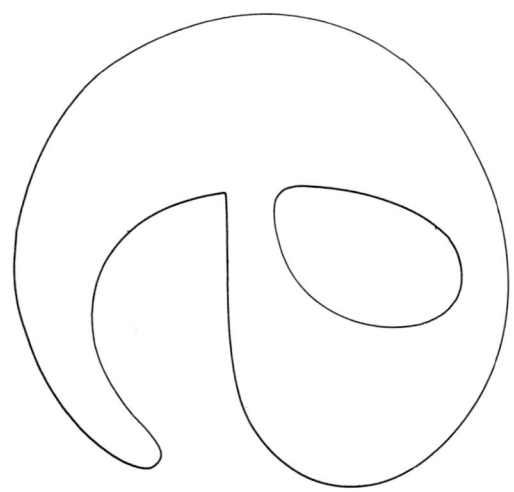

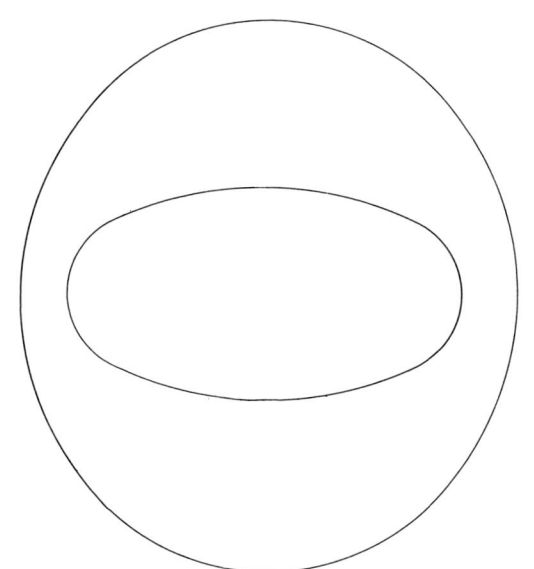

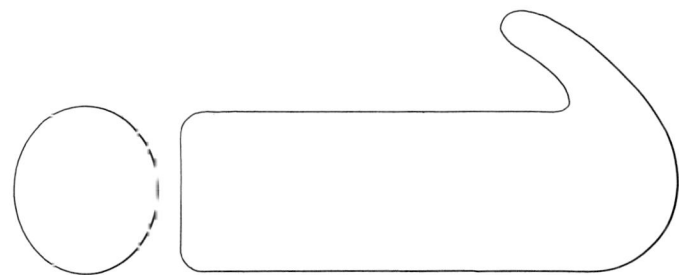

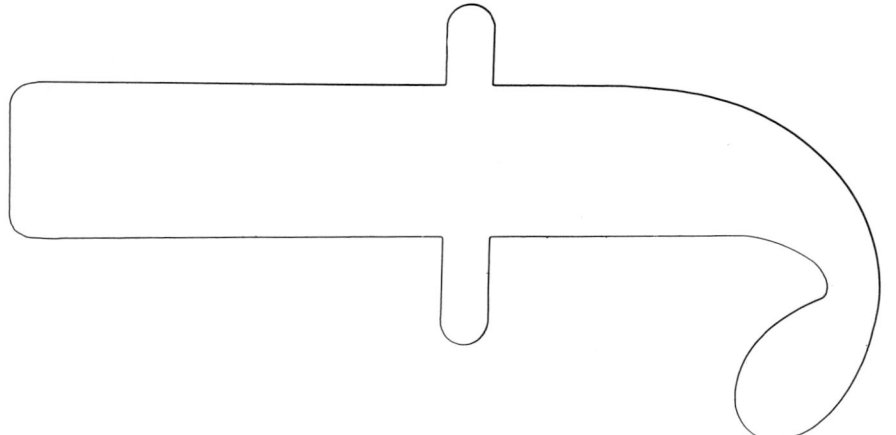

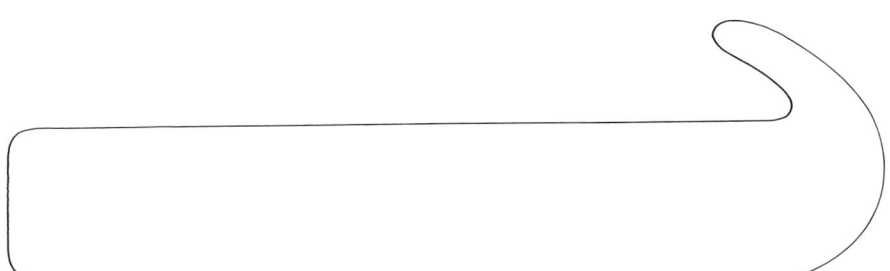

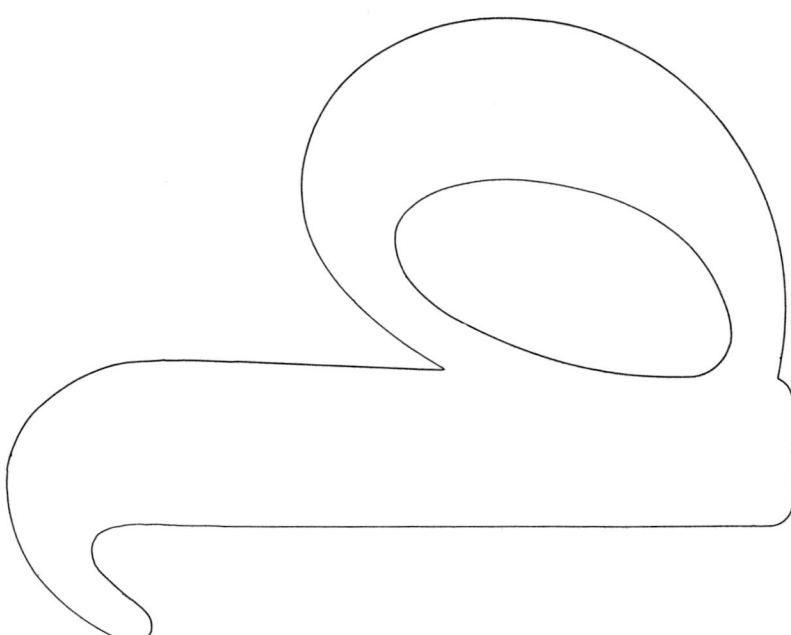
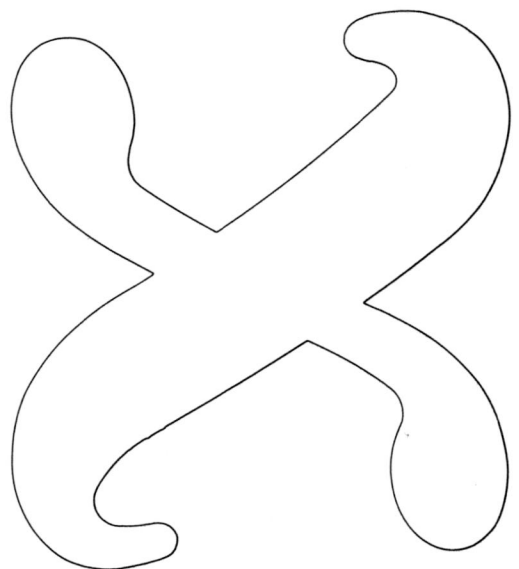

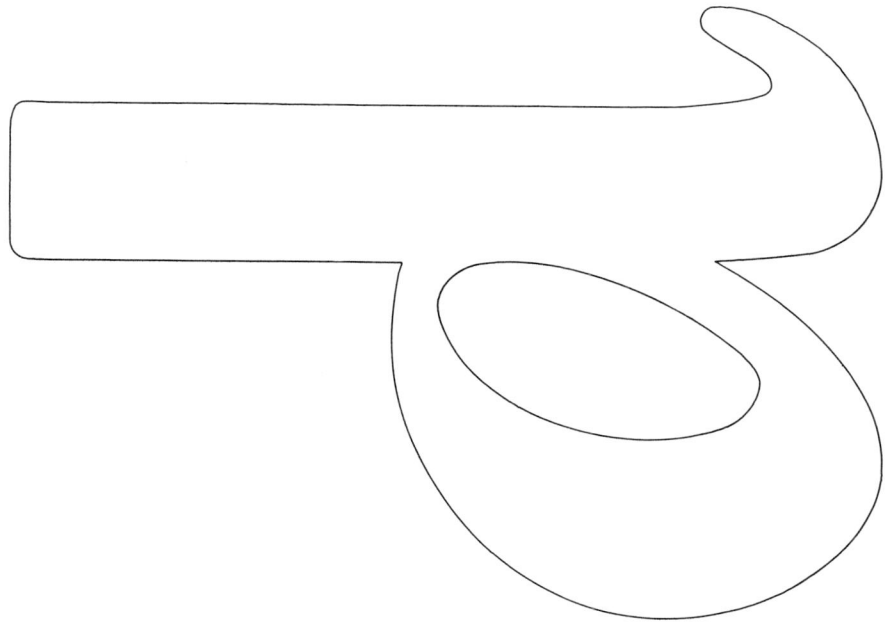

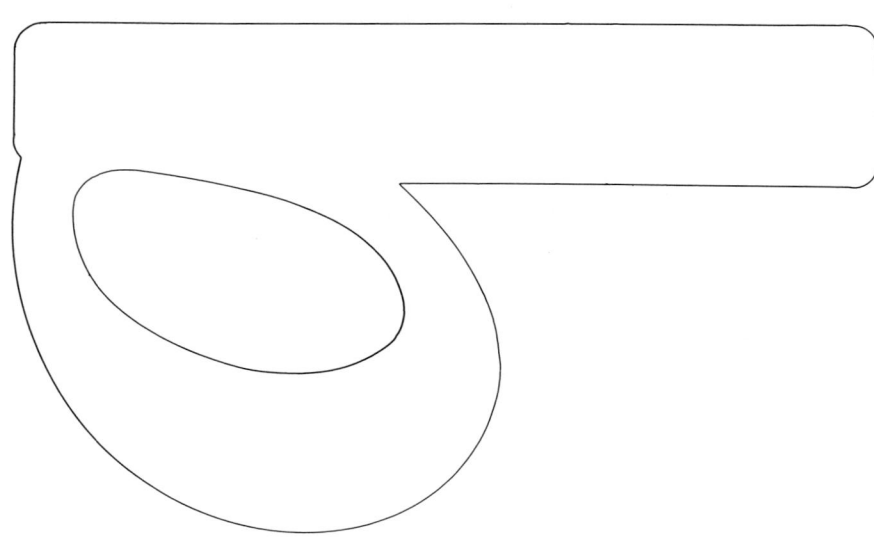
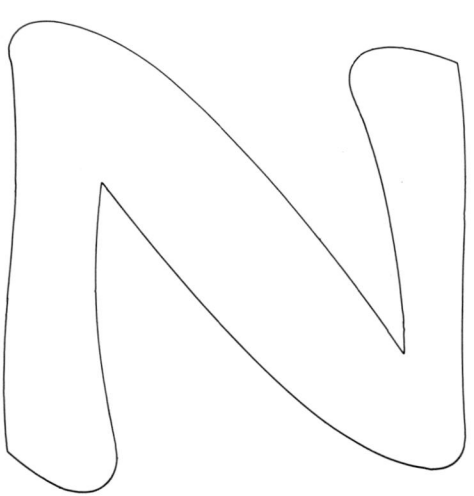

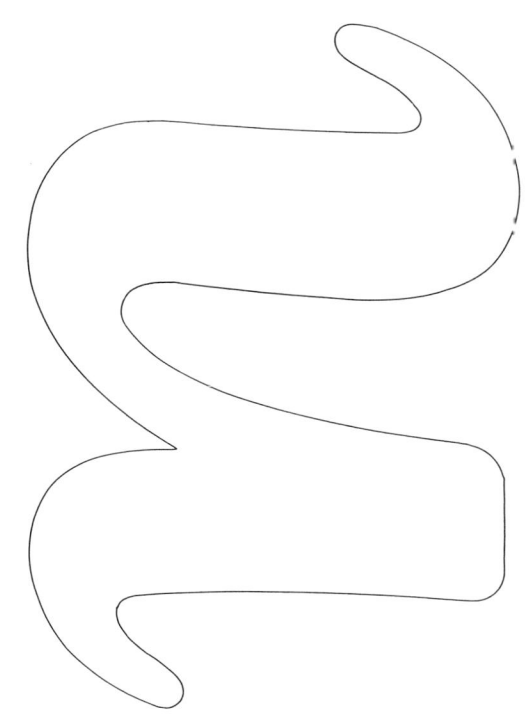

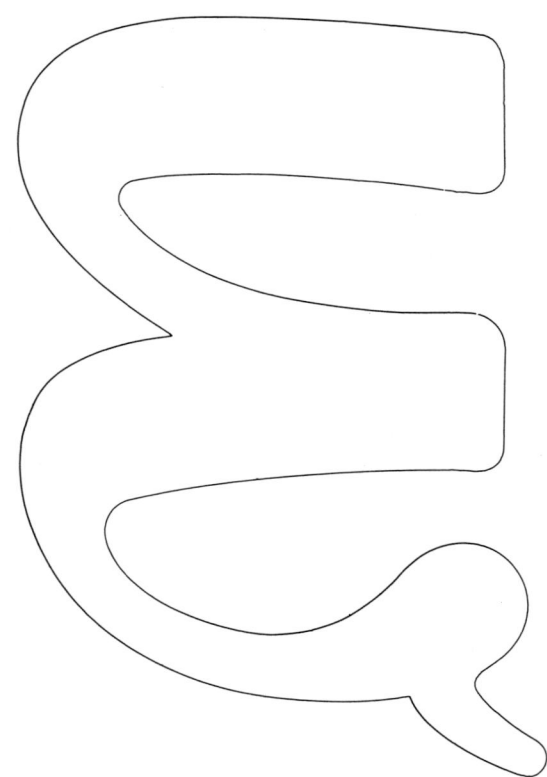

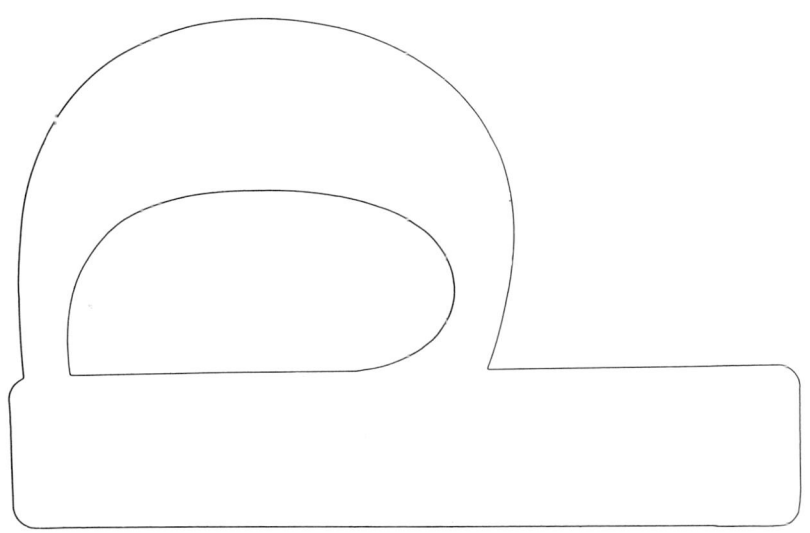
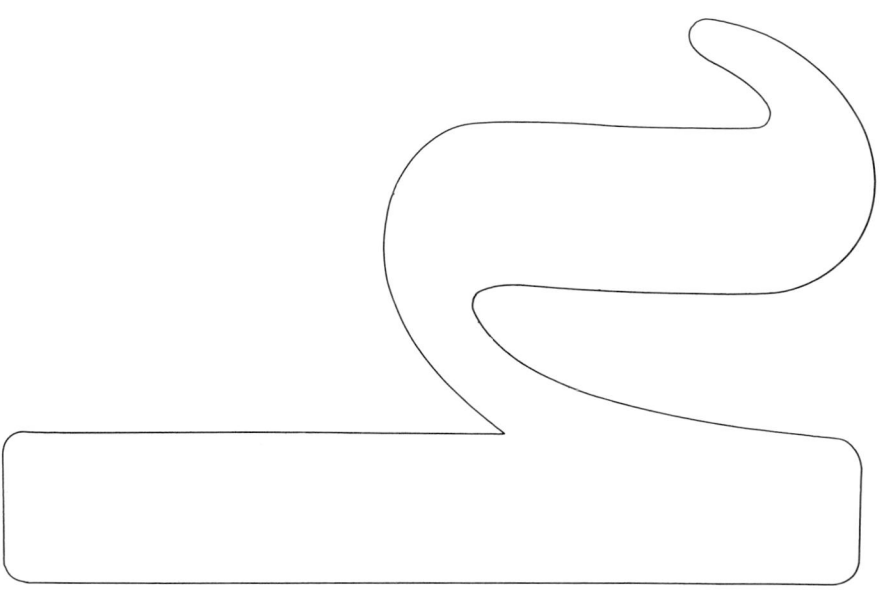

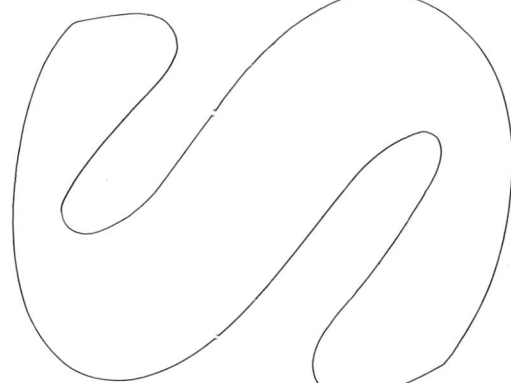
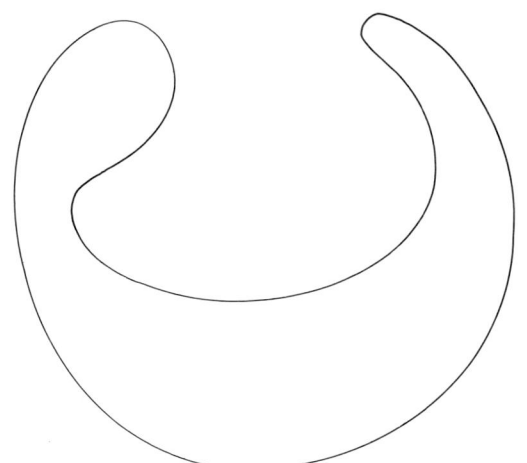

P-26-n   Copy this sheet on pink paper.

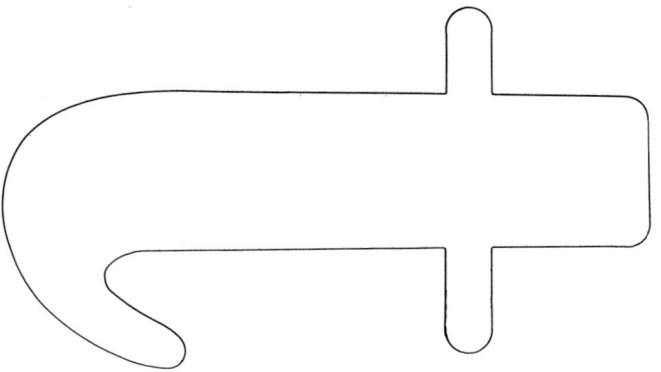

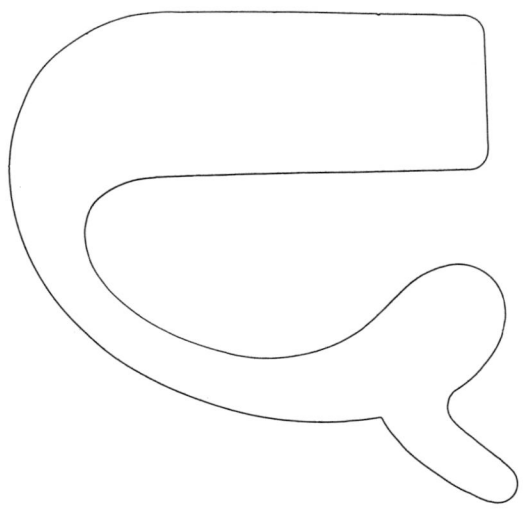

P-32-1 Copy this sheet on pink paper.

January	May
February	June
March	July
April	August

September	October	November	December
desk	flag	map	rug
mat	plant	bell	mug

Copy this sheet on white paper.

Saturday	Wednesday
Sunday	Thursday
Monday	Friday
Tuesday	

box	pen	pot	clip
dustpan	basket	basin	tank
inset	leg	lid	cup
tack	kid	clock	rack

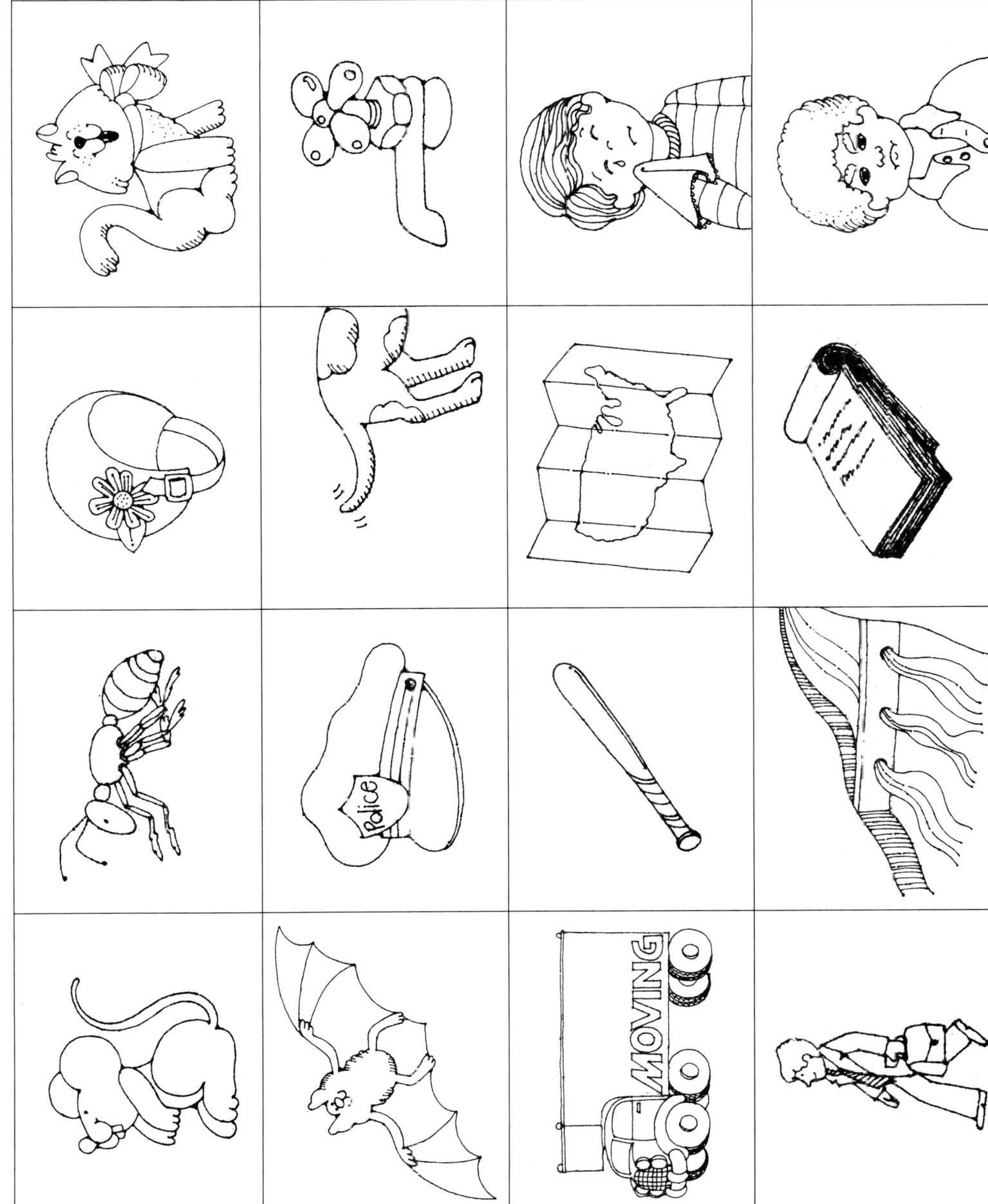

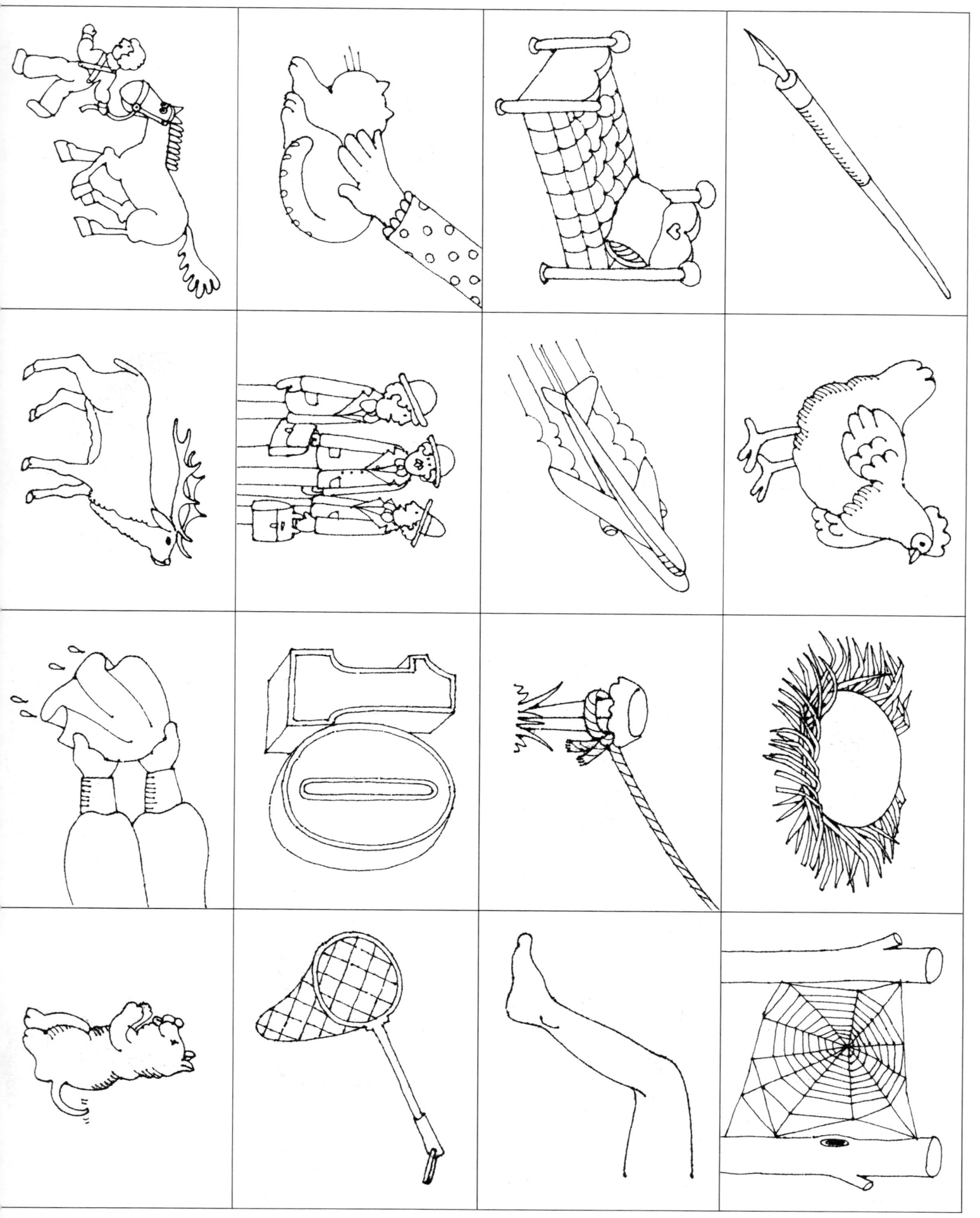

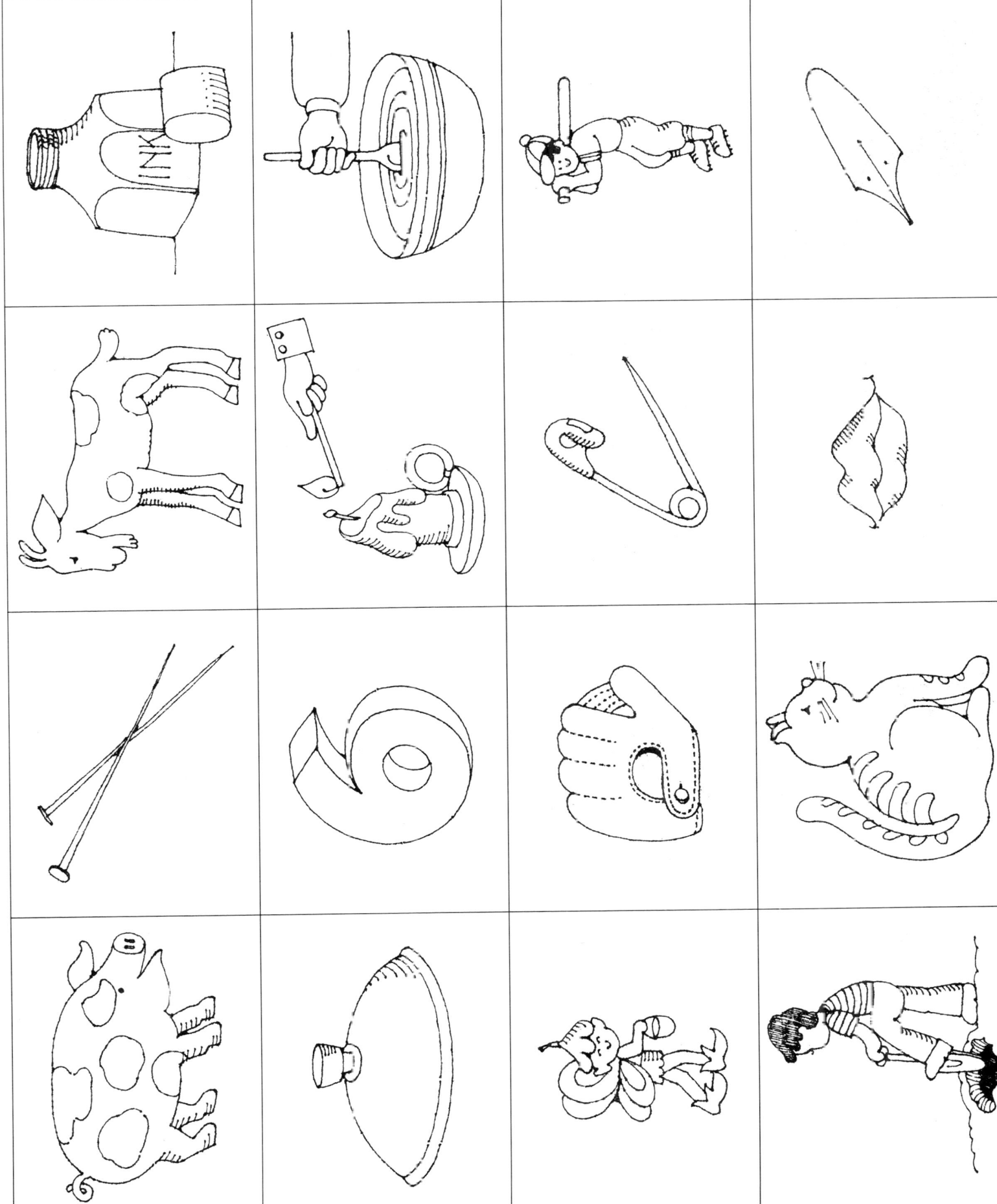

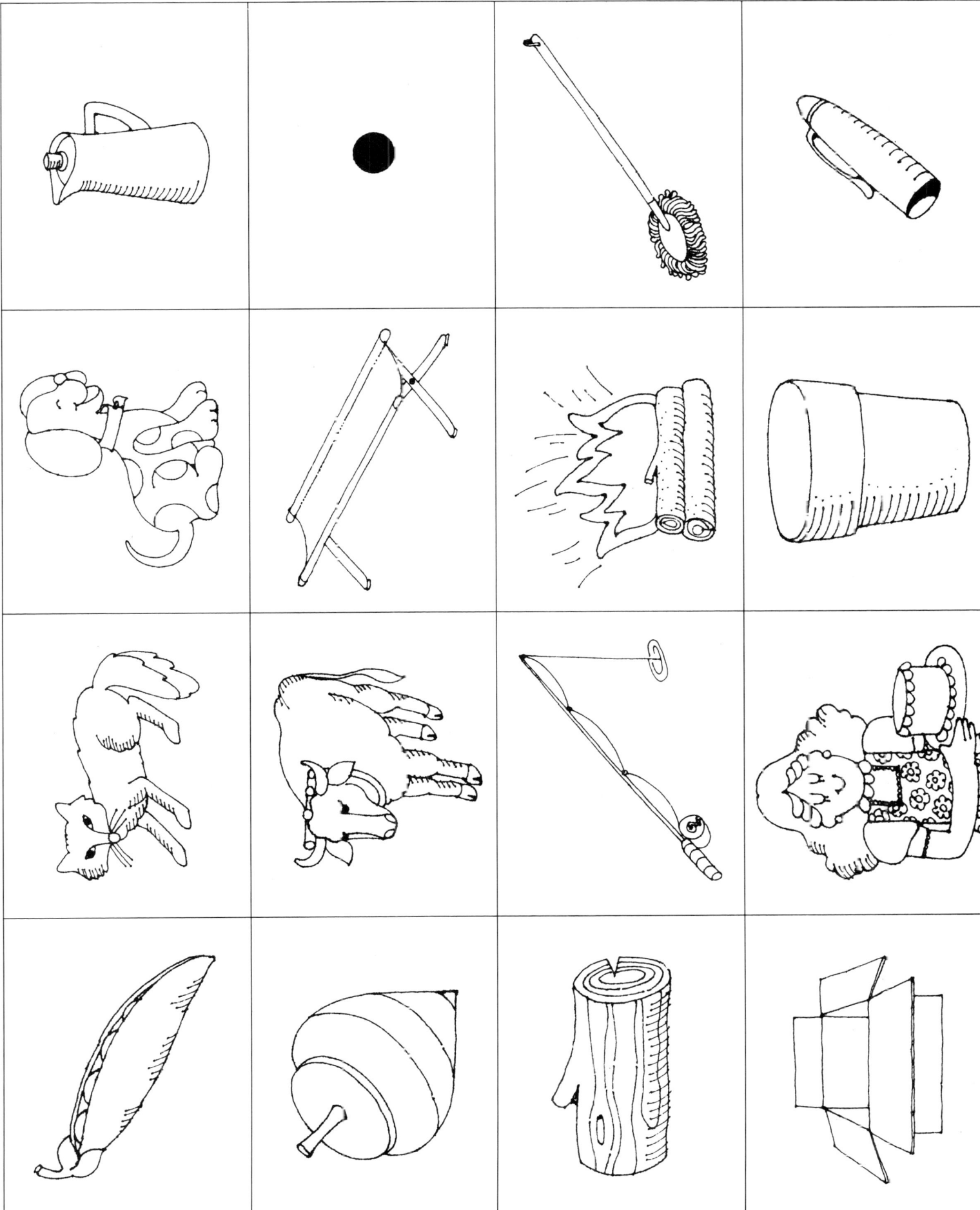

pot	fan	fox	mug
pig	pin	bug	elk
hen	dog	jet	hat
cat	cup	nib	lid

flag	button	kitten	ribbon
skull	bell	doll	frog
drum	twig	felt	rabbit
cross	sock	duck	stamp

ten	ton	keg	wig
wet	wig	sit	tip
pop	rag	rap	pot
rod	run	sap	tag

cat	Nan	hop	kit
pet	Dan	top	lad
nib	ink	hug	led
ram	bag	jam	lip

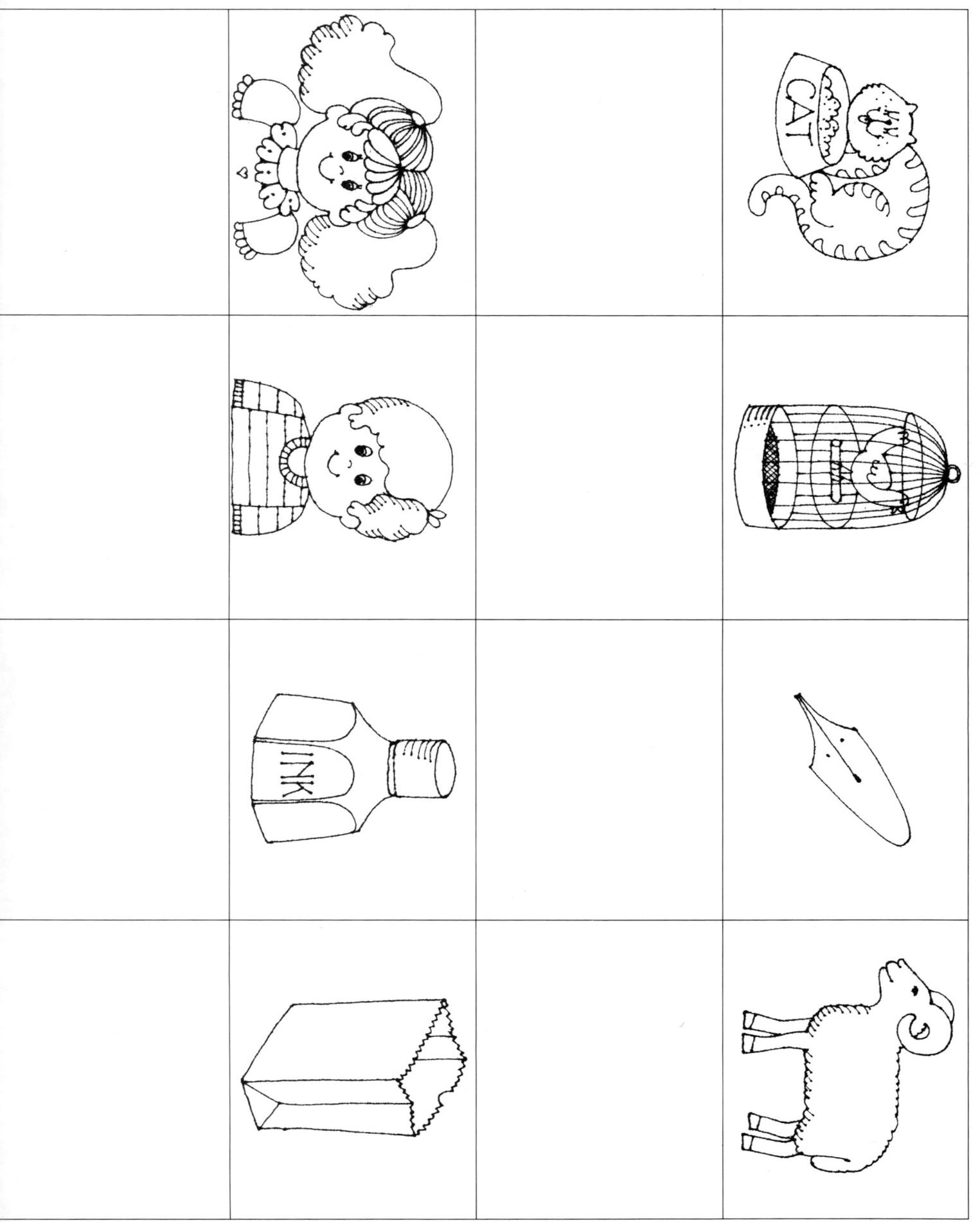

map	pen	lit	fat
bus	bat	web	dam
man	dad	elm	leg
mom	men	sad	pad

P-46-1 Copy this sheet on pink paper.

dog	beg	pod	imp
hen	bud	pat	van
ax	rat	pet	mix
bag	cat	pup	cut

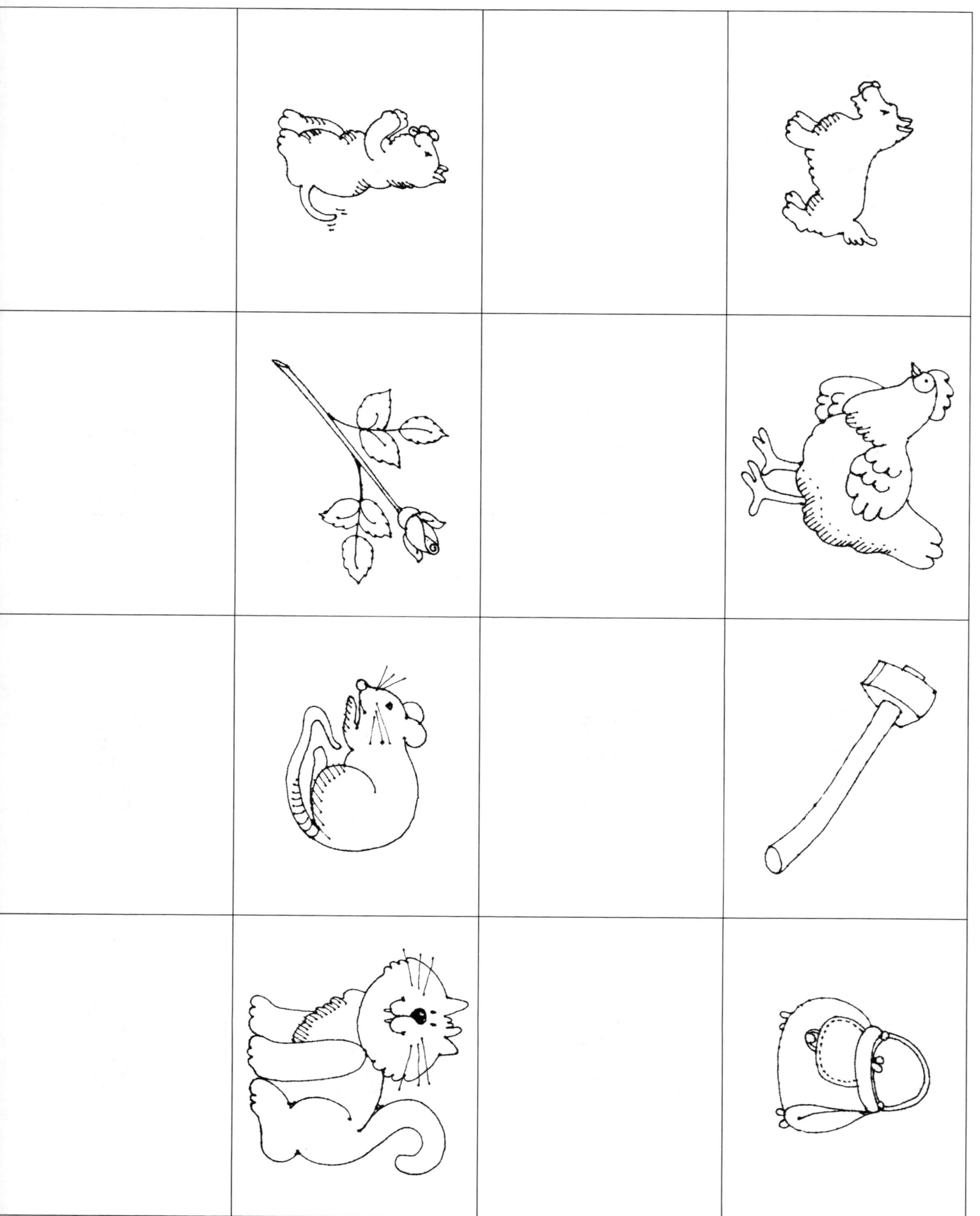

bat	hat	gun	fan
bun	mug	hut	dig
mad	mat	mud	nap
ox	pan	pin	pit

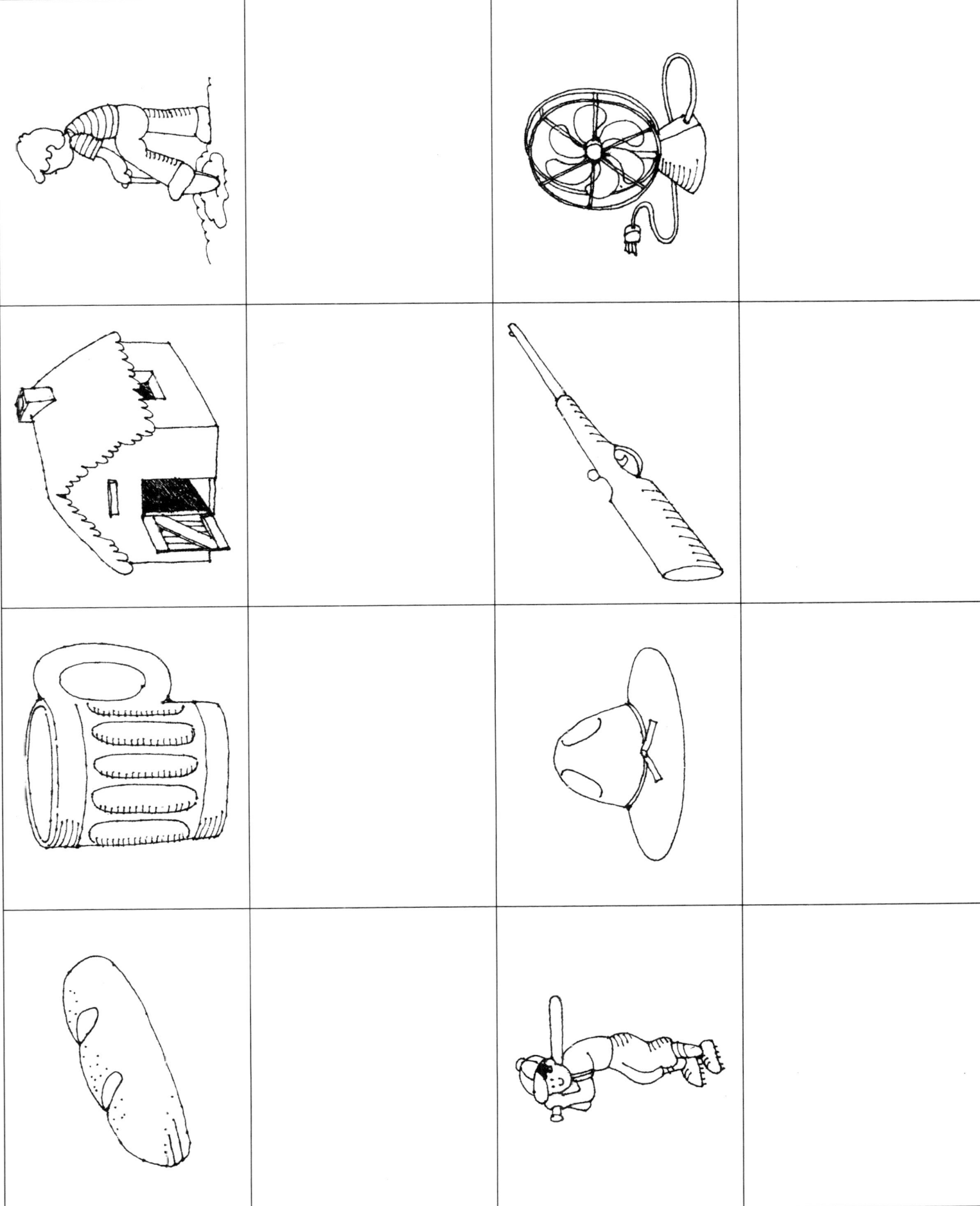

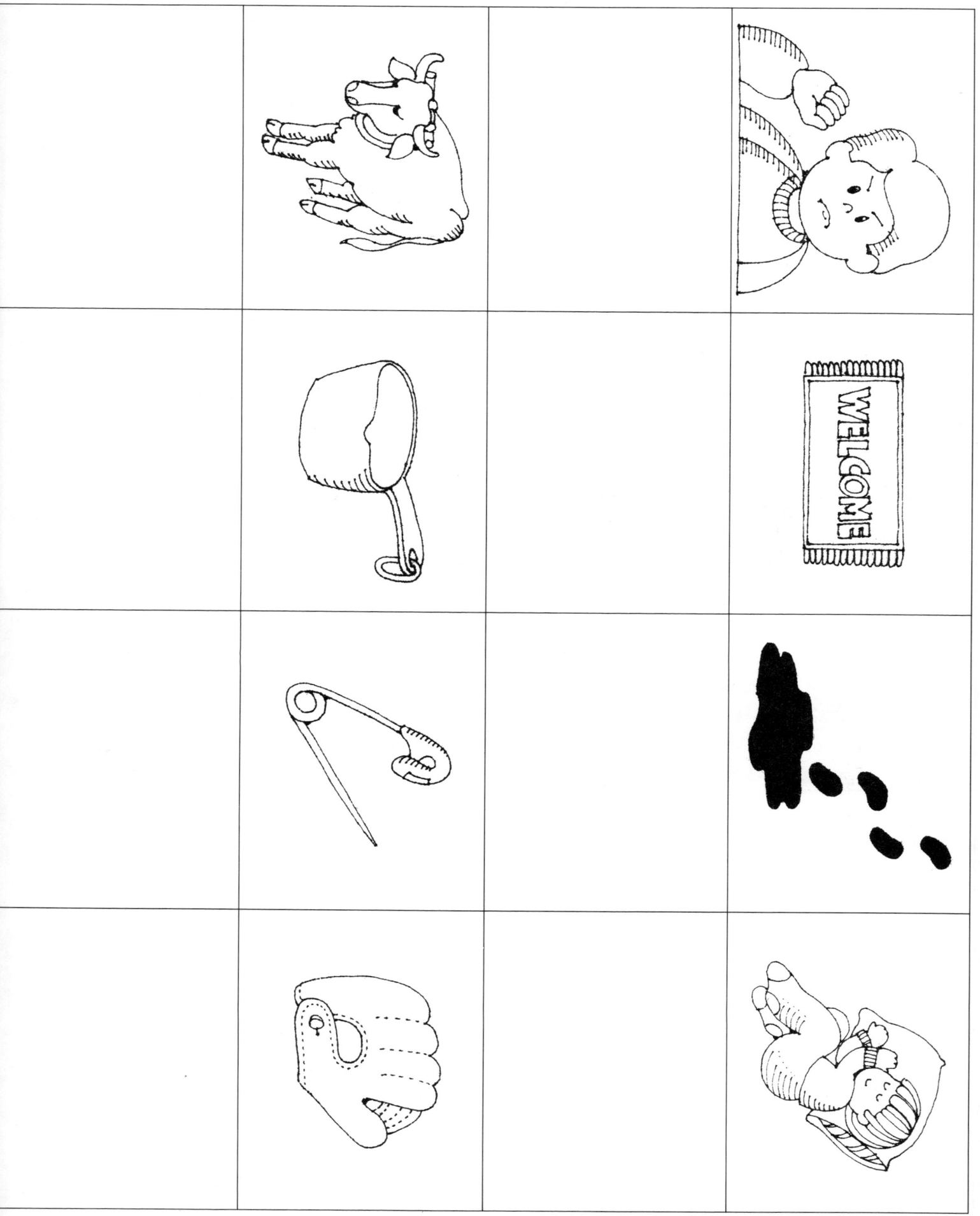

fan	gum	pan	rug
bug	kid	log	cap

ant	hat	six	cup
pig	bat	lid	box

	tub		egg
	nut		elk
	van		can
	fox		sun

mop	net	top	tub
jet	tap	jug	pup

noun	noun	noun	noun
verb	verb	verb	verb
verb	article	article	adjective
adjective	verb	singular	plural

noun	verb	verb	adjective
noun	verb	article	verb
noun	verb	article	singular
noun	verb	adjective	plural

pen	hen	bag	egg
cat	man	mom	Nan
dog	fox	dad	kid
ram	mud	hog	pig

cock	sack	kitten	well
milk	land	duckling	skunk
duck	rabbit	piglet	frog
bull	grass	wagon	pond

nag	fan	mad	run
tap	gag	rap	yap
beg	pet	dig	sit
hit	jig	sip	nod

snap	kick	skip	limp
clap	rest	sing	plod
bang	fret	wink	flop
bend	grin	swim	drum

this	that	they	was
I	the	are	is

one	you	two	who
my	girl	they	what

to	their	were	there
where	enough	laugh	friend

a	a	a	a
a	a	a	a
the	a	a	a
the	a	a	a

the	the	an	an
the	the	an	an
the	the	an	an
the	the	an	an

wet	tin	dim	top
six	ten	fat	sad
bad	mad	big	odd
red	hot	big	fat

stiff	pink	spotted	black
lost	cotton	plump	best
bent	rotten	soft	grim
damp	gruff	timid	still

tap	bad
let	yes
pip	vim
ox	cod
sum	hum
ham	had
get	hem
bib	big
dot	bog
dug	sip

and	at
peg	elf
dim	fit
sod	sop
but	rug
had	ran
egg	leg
fit	did
cot	cod
bun	bus

yap	am
hen	pen
is	did
off	pop
hug	tug
fat	ham
beg	wet
fin	lip
jog	job
bug	cup

lap	rap
wed	end
big	nip
not	on
pun	rut
add	yap
vex	red
din	rim
rob	got
sup	cup

tax	gap
yet	let
wet	gig
win	lot
hog	rum
mud	gag
has	vet
met	bet
hid	not
us	up

clip	rock	clips	rocks
pin	stamp	pins	stamps
band	tack	bands	tacks
ring	nib	nibs	rings

ran	run	sit	hop
sat	fed	tug	cut
mop	is	is	is
was	not	not	not

pet	hum	got	nip
led	tap	jog	fit
was	nag	dug	fix
sip	pat	rub	got

has	has	can	can
did	did	will	bat
had	wag	fed	led
get	met	hid	bit

sent	drink	drinking	drinks
kept	happen	sitting	rest
smelled	buzz	standing	rests
rested	fussed	stands	stand

lost	glad	mend	send
felt	fell	bring	fling
drops	went	skips	fled
tell	slap	puffed	twist

trotting	romp	trots	will
grunting	vexed	slept	will
hissing	hisses	trot	grunts
tapping	wept	crept	lept

puff	bump	kiss	sits
huff	hiss	laps	dust
yell	snip	jump	hops
cannot	pulling	pulls	running

fox	can	can	can
lad	bug	ring	ring
pin	pin	pin	lad
nut	nut	nut	nut

vet

elf

Ben

get

net

leg

hen

egg

at

gas

as

act

rag

add

jam

sap

run

rut

nun

us

tip

lip

fit

him

rod

wit

mop

fin

jot

bum

rob

sum

end

six

jet

wig

sit

fix

dig

mix

Bend a leg.

Dust a box.

Get a drink.

Rest on a rug.

Pick up a pin.

Jump up.

Dust a plant.

Pick up a box.

Pick up a rug.

Clap a song.

Sing a song.

Get a snack.

Fill a cup.

Get a rug.

Sit on a rug.

Lift a leg.

Lift a hand.

Lift a lid.

Get a pen.

Hang a hat.

Sit and hum.

Pick up a pin.

Stand and hop.

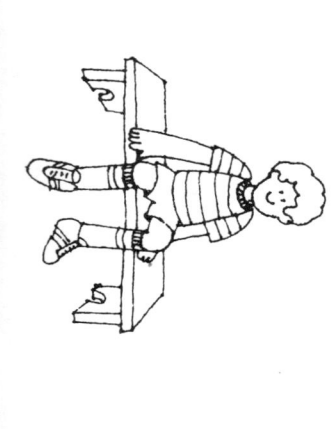		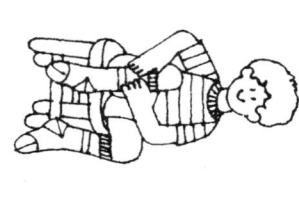	
Ed sits in the red sox.	Ed hits in his red sox.	Ed pulls on his red sox.	Ed has red sox.

Ed jumps in red sox.

Ed bats in his red sox.

Ed runs in his red sox.

Ed wins in his red sox.

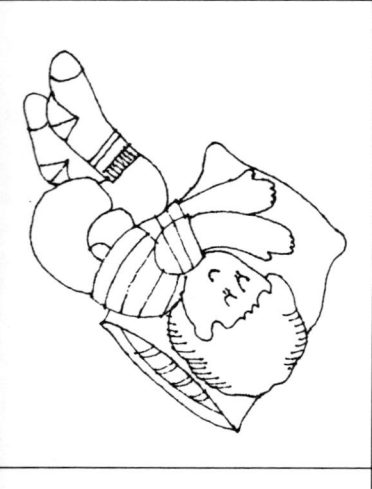	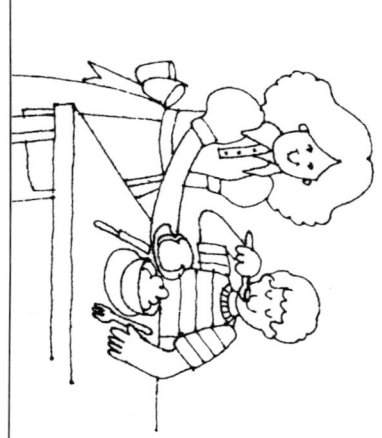	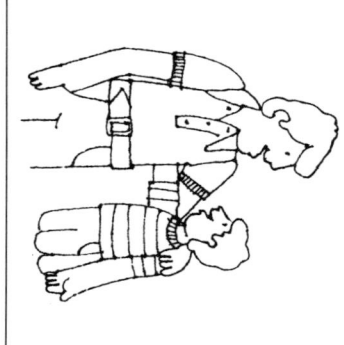	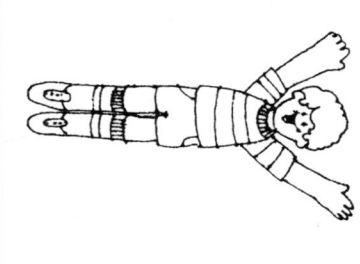
Ed naps in his red sox.	Mom fed Ed.	Dad gets Ed.	Ed felt grand in red sox.

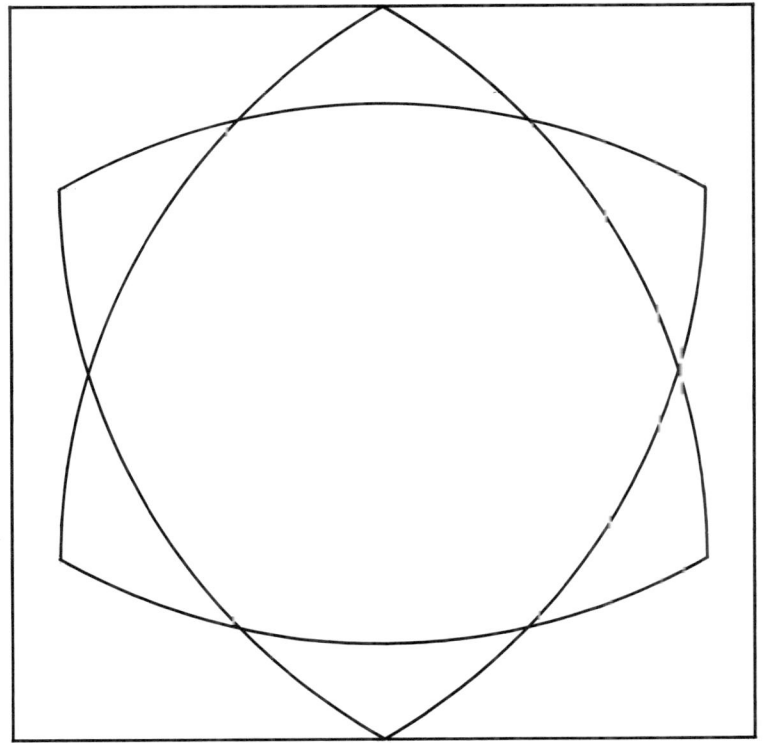

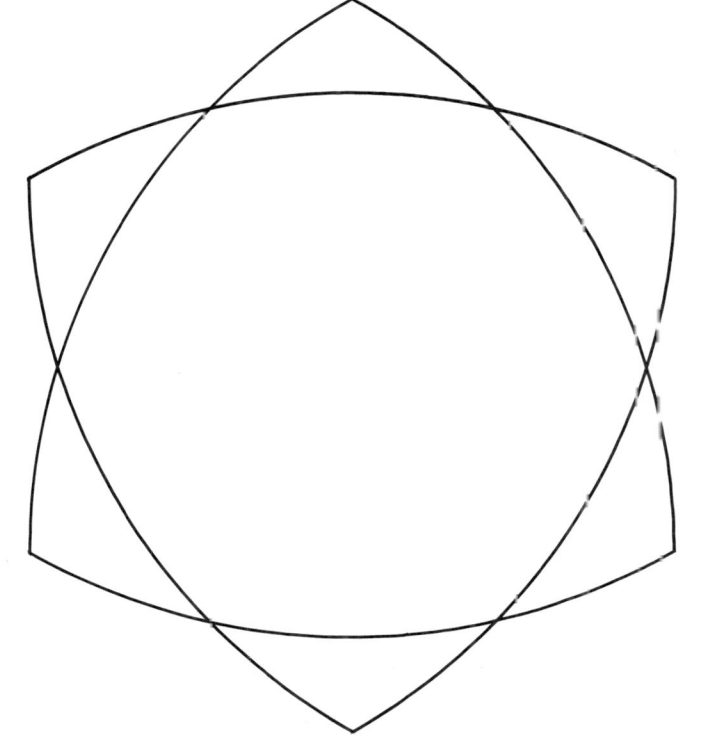

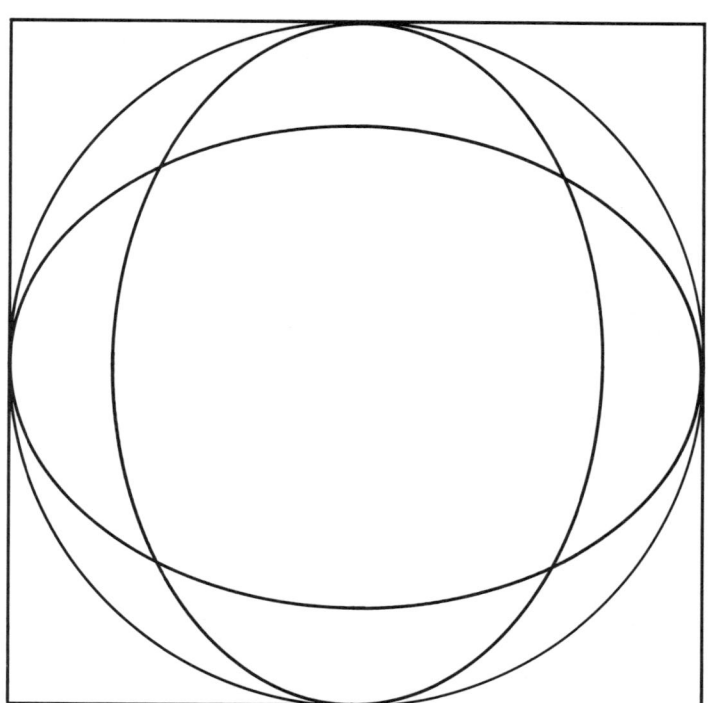

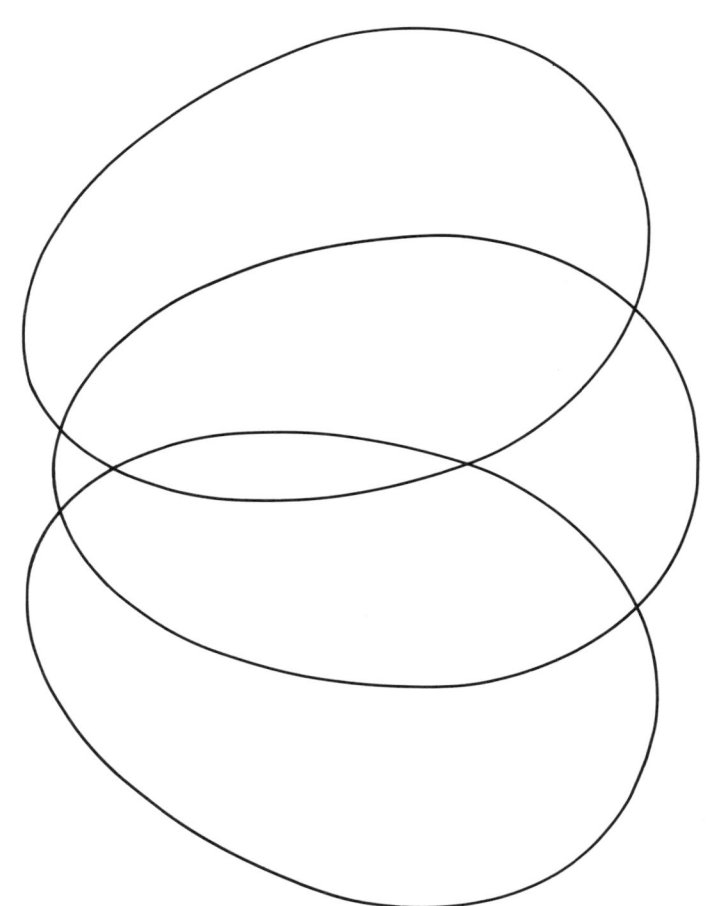

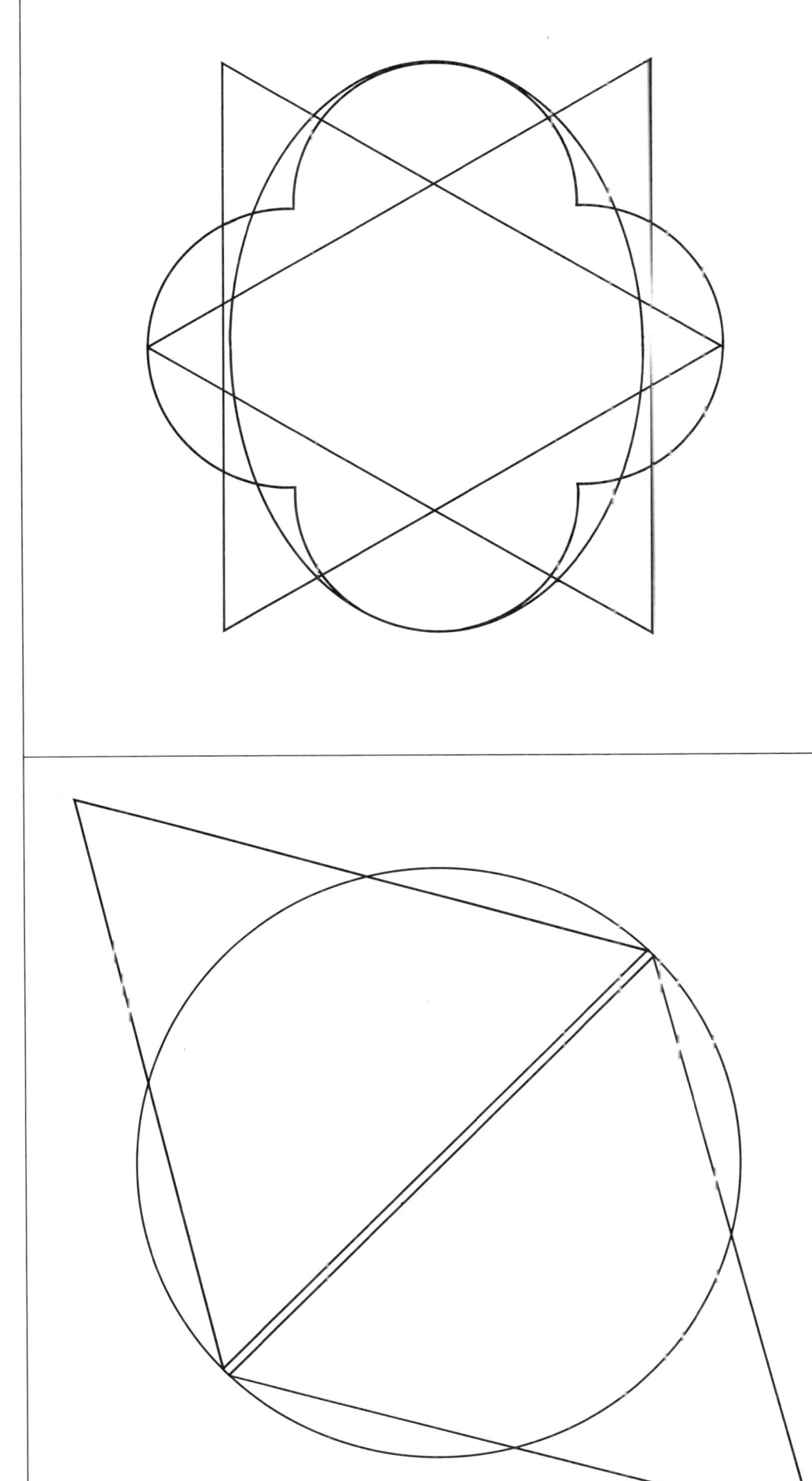

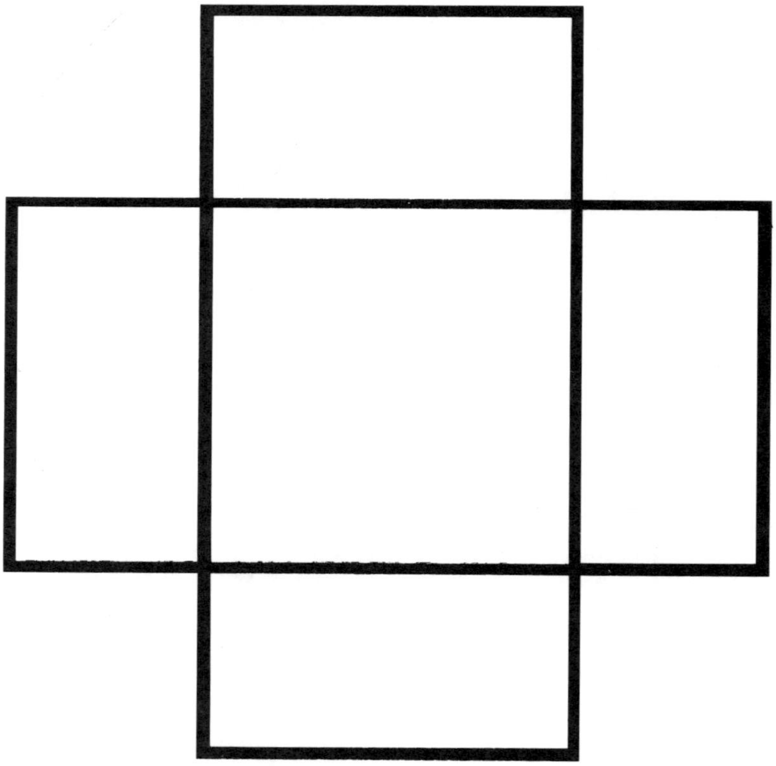

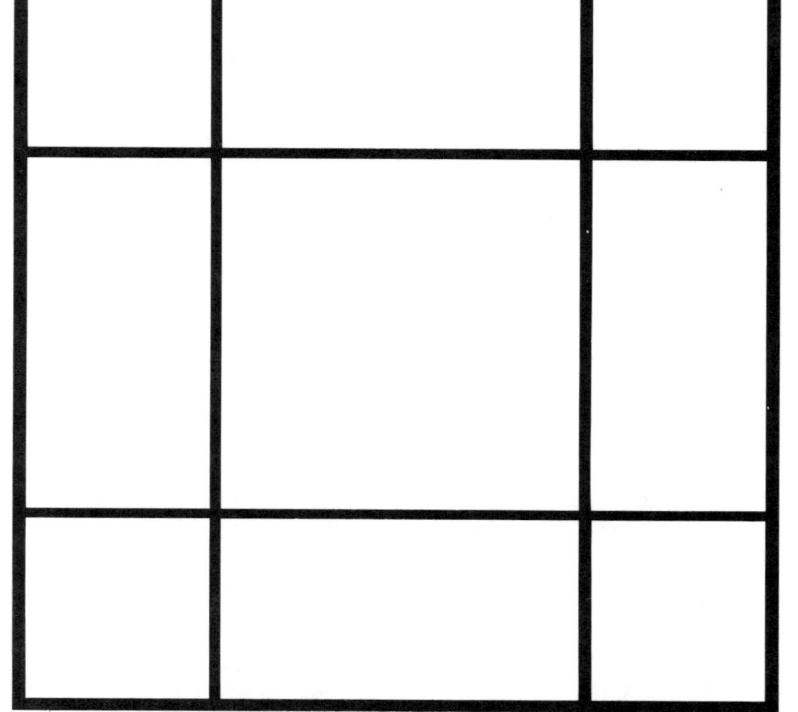

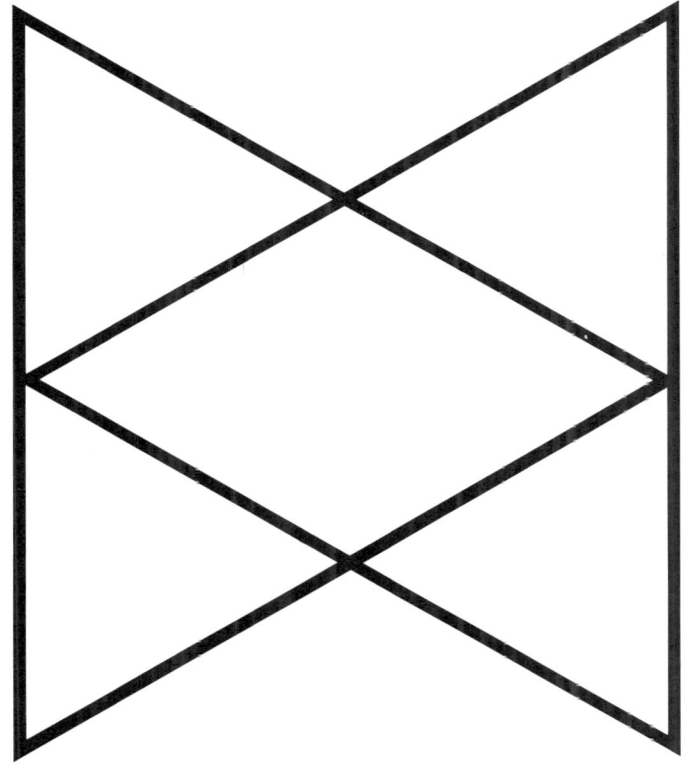

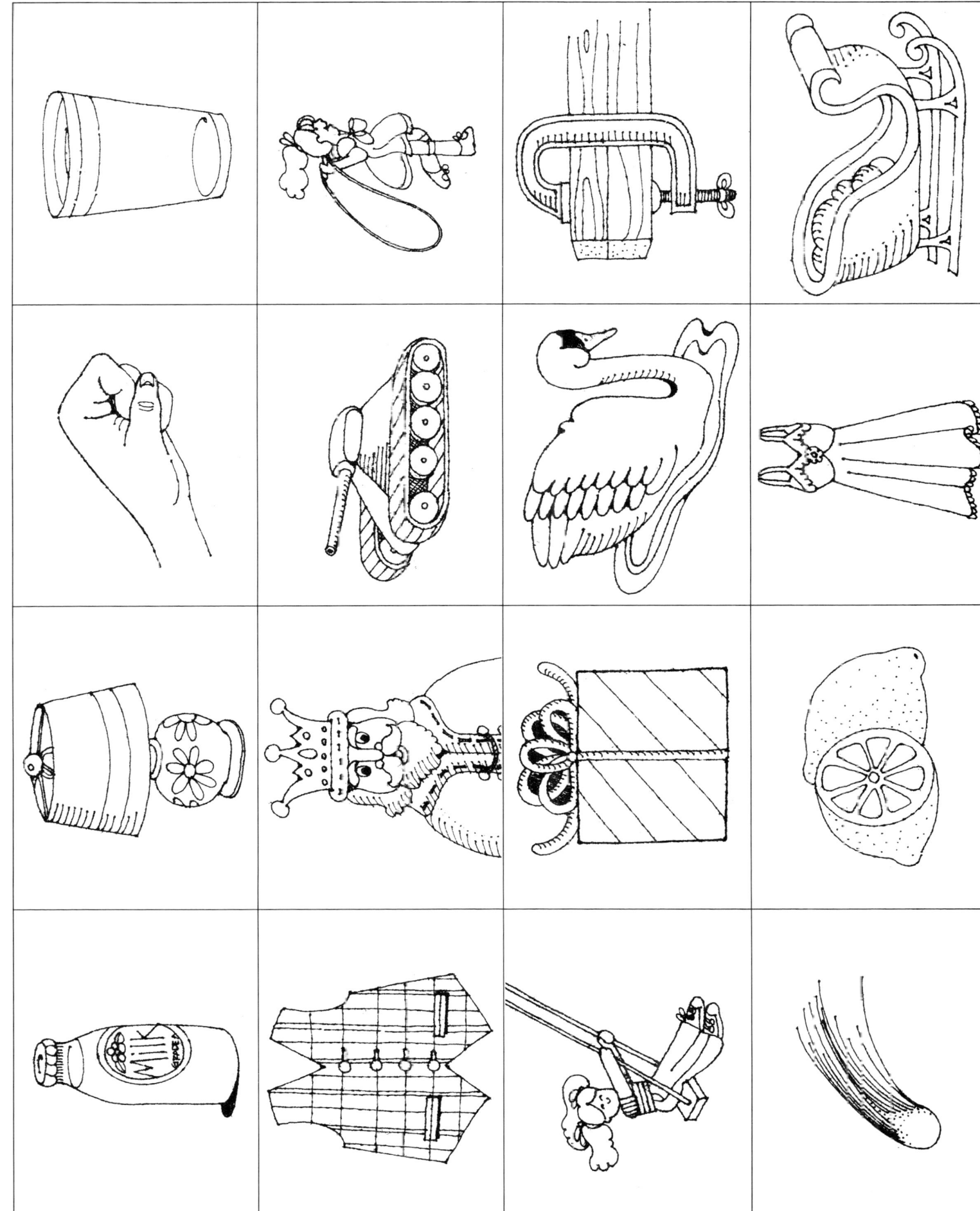

claps	bulb	clip	mask
flag	umbrella	hang	sled
Fran	duck	Jack	glasses
rabbit	crab	lock	stamp

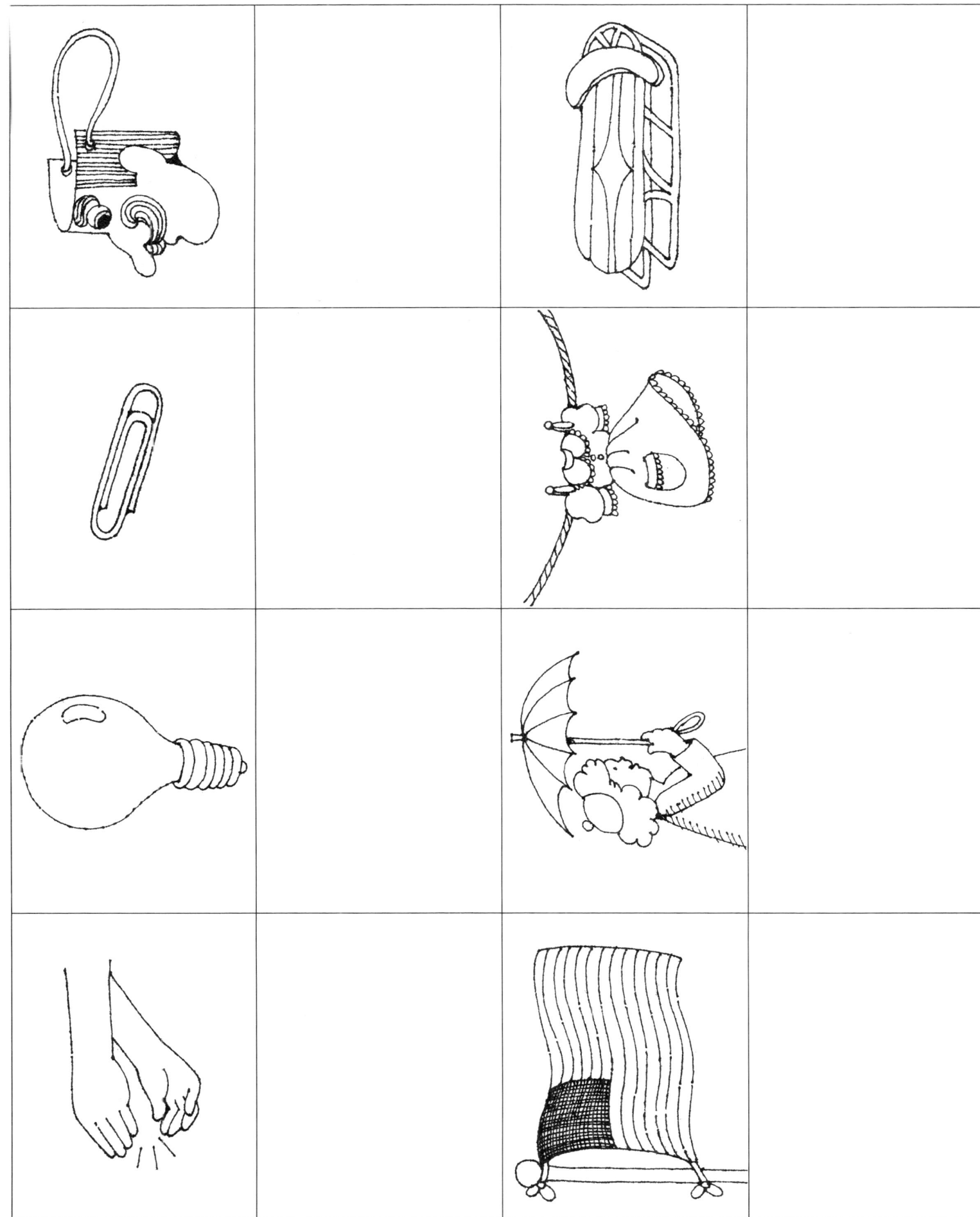

bulb	sled	camel	mask
hang	umbrella	sink	flag
stamp	clubs	drink	skip
crab	napkin	bonnet	clap

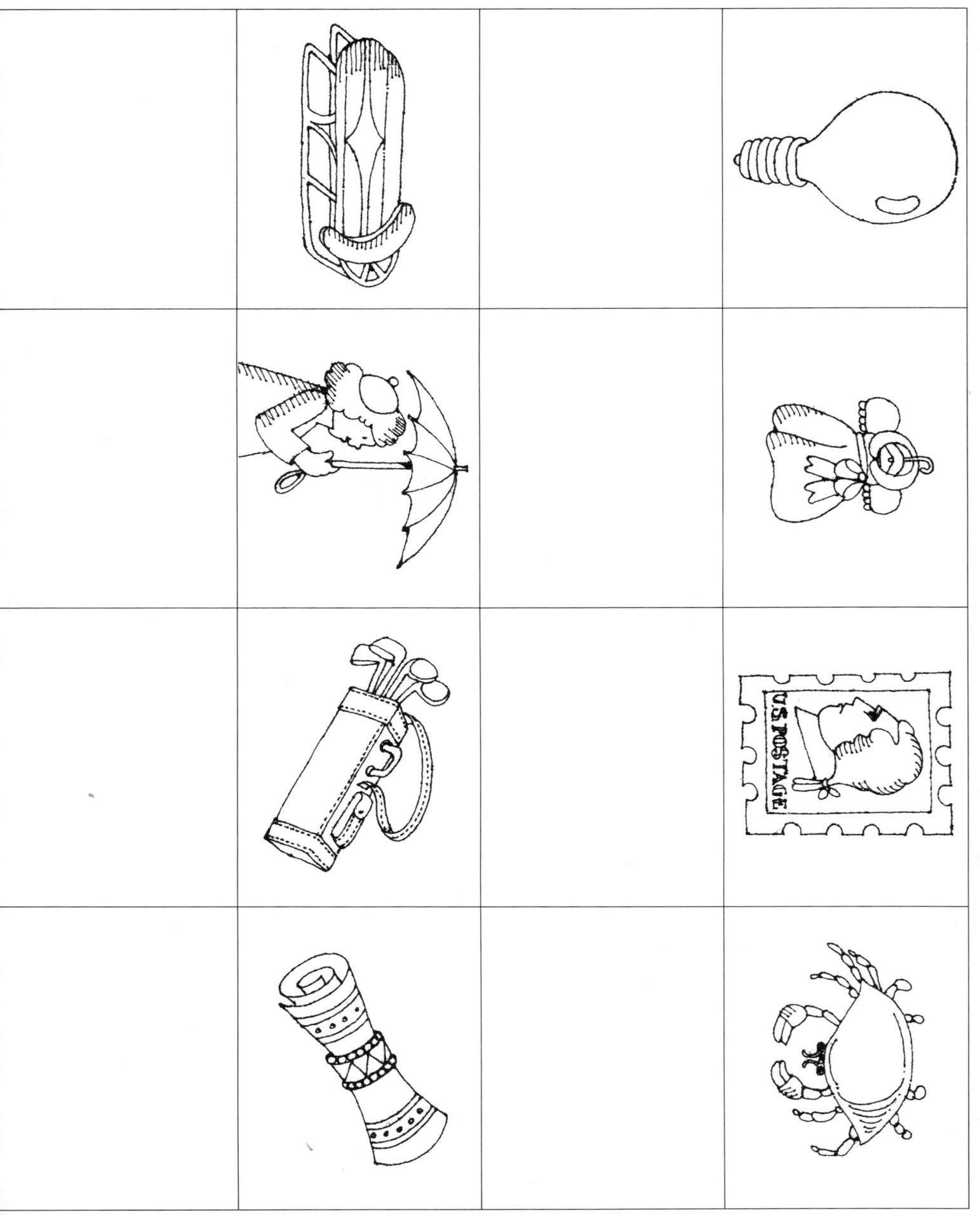

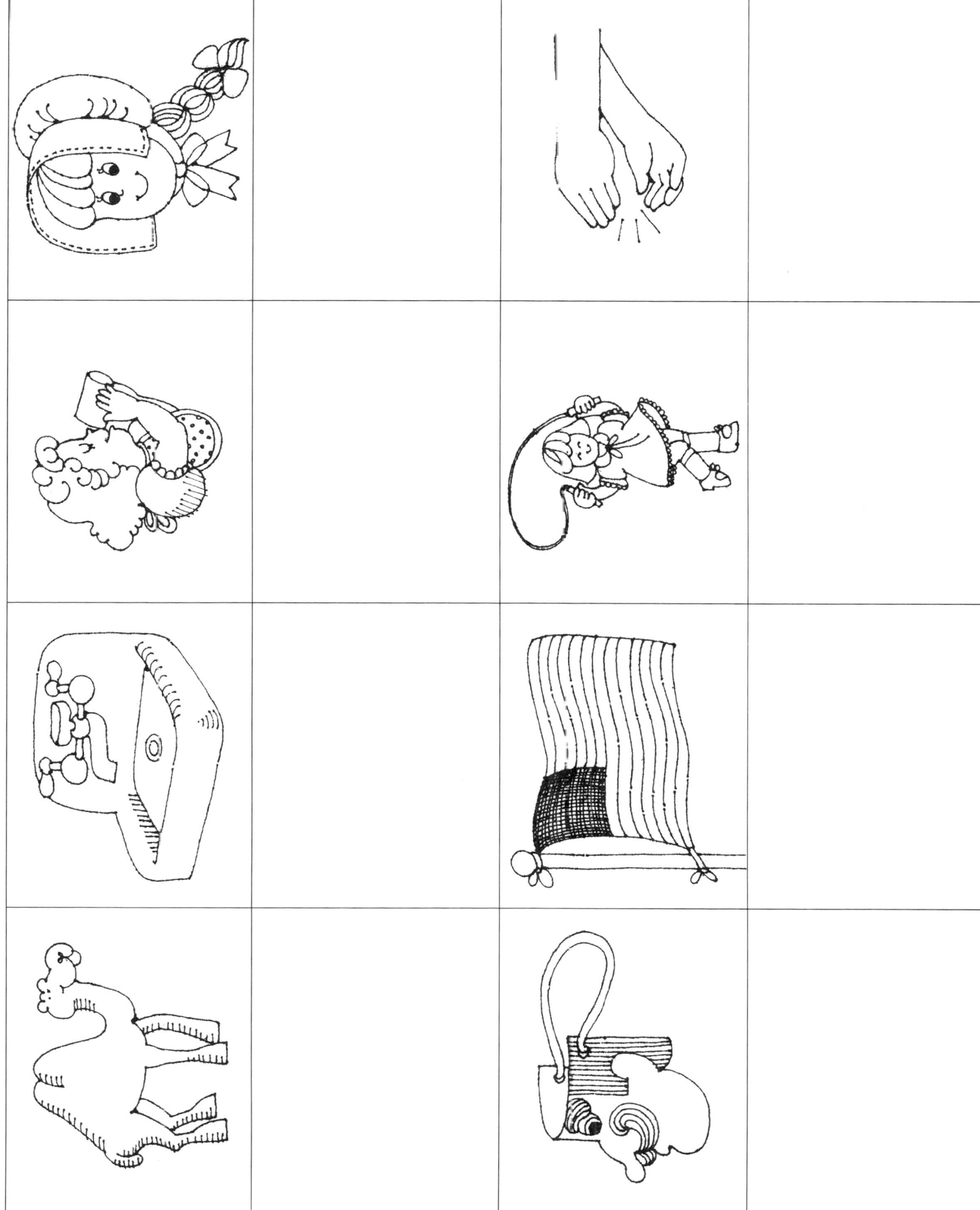

flag	umbrella	mask	sink
sled	hand	camp	bulb
pumpkin	mitten	tacks	hand
Donna	camp	belt	clock

lock	napkin	sack	sampan
gift	milk	comet	crib
rocks	swing	cross	clamp
tent	sock	lemon	cock

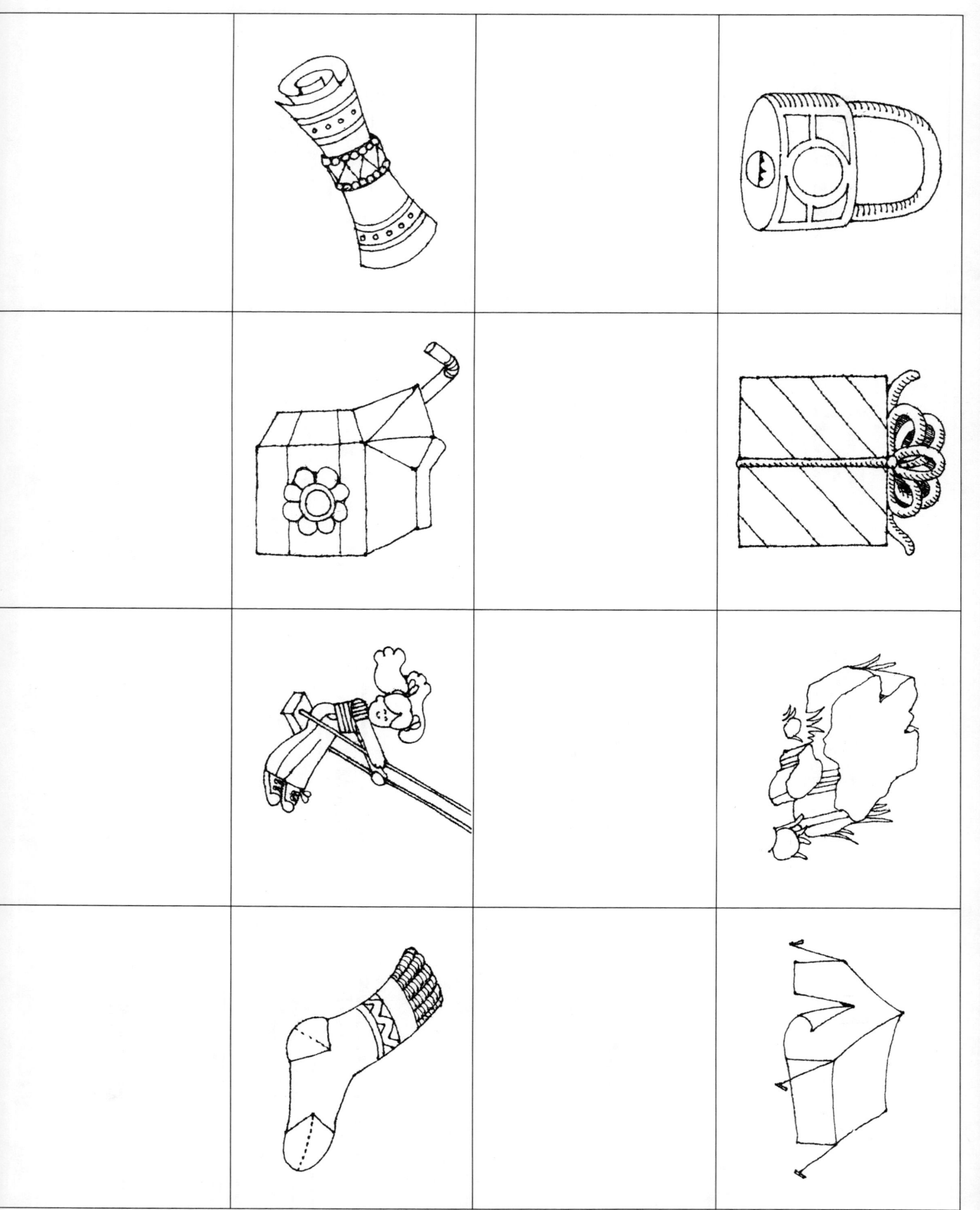

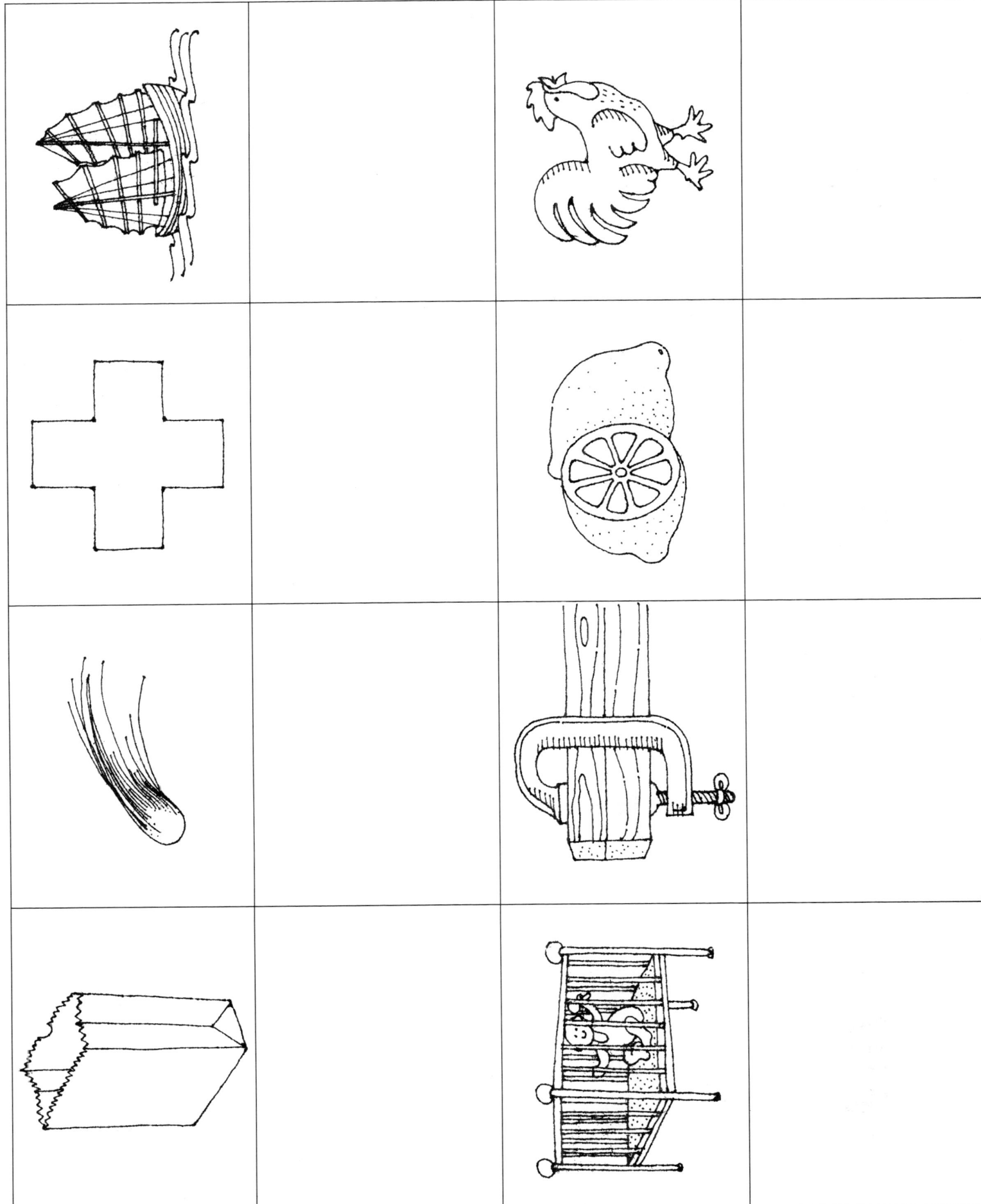

steps	skip	sled	sink
slip	trap	drink	camel
skunk	basket	spuds	plum
tickets	desk	frock	swan

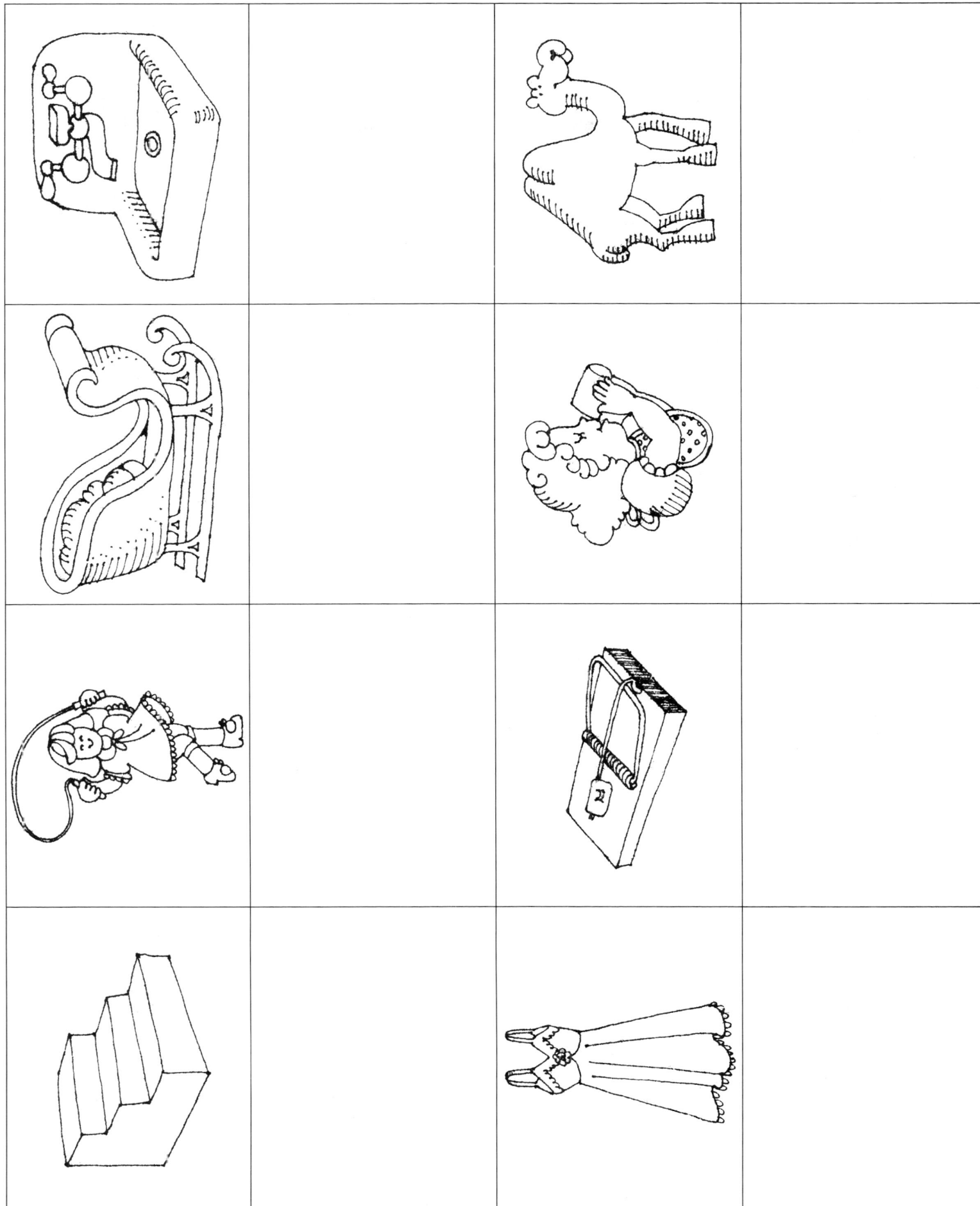

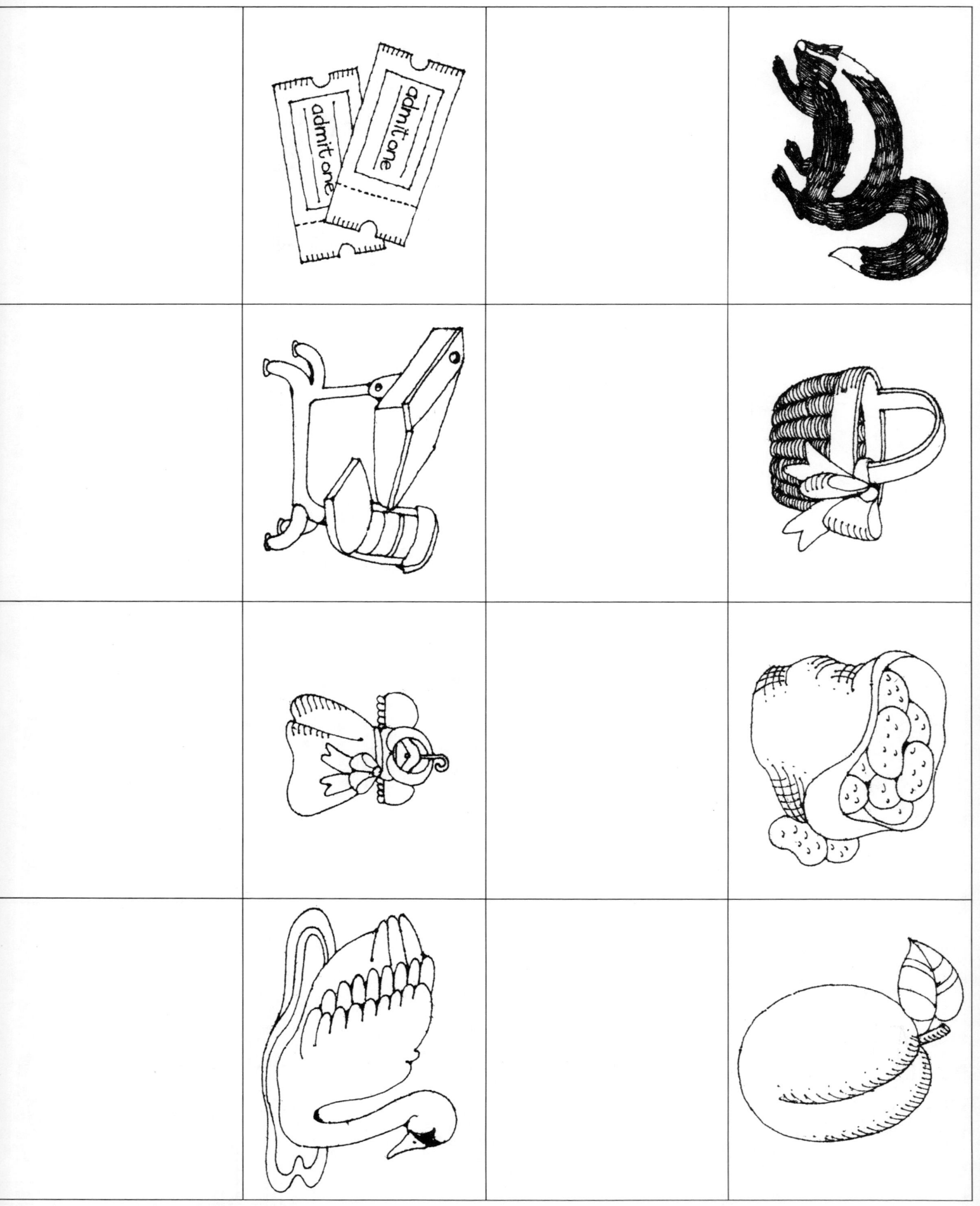

| club | ring | bell | swing |
| compass | button | sack | clam |

kitten		sack
frog		clock
milk		drum
lamp		nest

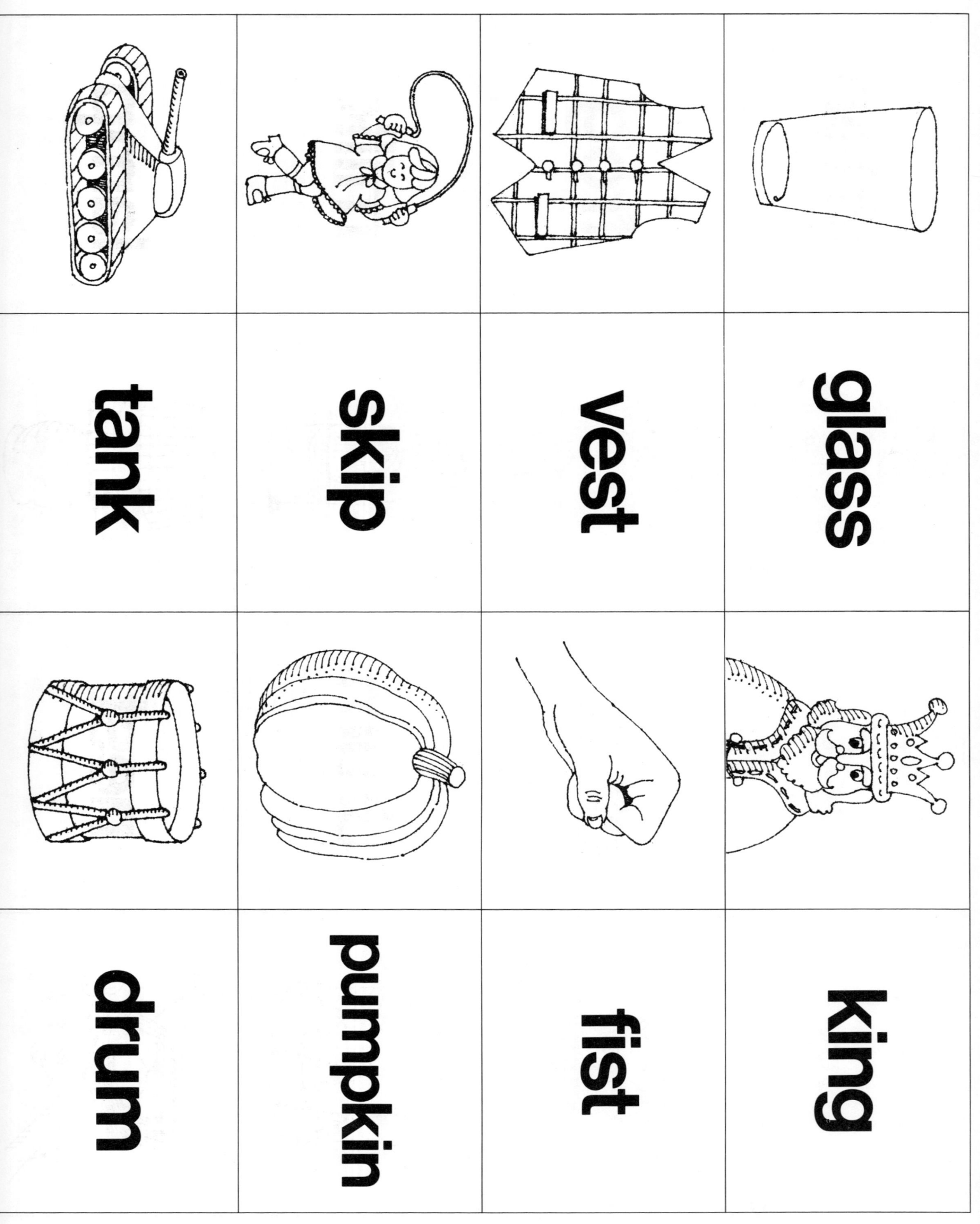

bent	hump
land	insist
windmill	timid
picnic	expect
stop	swag
glum	velvet
madcap	bled
strand	hubbub
grin	punt
helmet	blond

expand	slim
from	plug
held	gulp
wept	handbag
best	inhibit
vivid	cutup
trot	rumpus
drop	strap
spirit	must
fond	spot

hulk	bust
crop	limp
swan	grim
trip	risk
lend	fund
sent	eldest
west	just
prim	neglect
send	wept
drag	spin

dump

fled

bond

hint

grin

spin

trot

hundrum

strand

brat

grab

swum

yelp

fond

snug

bulk

prop

skin

lump

fret

B-93-d Copy this sheet on blue paper.

self	brim
slit	prop
fond	tint
slot	lisp
trap	clog
scram	stag
glub	plod
brag	sandman
lump	hotspot
clot	stab

from	drop
trod	Scot

stun

tusk

hunt

fund

plod

crop

fond

flop

spit

twin

grip

slim

skid

brig

wind

silk

sent

melt

best

fled

Fred

lend

fret

held

cram	scan
stand	strand

slap

scat

snag

drab

gust

gulp

runt

snub